CW00493379

Spiritualist Venues

Edition 1

(updated April 2022)

Compiled by Veronica Jenkins

https://findmeamedium.com

https://www.facebook.com/findmeamedium1

https://www.etsy.com/uk/shop/SpiritualistGifts

Contents

Areas

Introduction

This book is basically a list of Spiritualist Venues across the UK. Currently this list contains details of 553 organisations which hold services at various types of locations including purpose built Churches, Quaker Meeting Halls, Masonic Lodges to community centres.

The Spiritualist organisations classify themselves as Churches, Centres and groups. Many of these Churches and Centres are affiliated to the Spiritualist National Union or the Greater World Christian Spiritualist Church Organisation but an increasingly large number of groups are independent of any central organisation and are run by local mediums/Spiritualists.

The organisations in this book all hold Spiritualist services or Evenings of Mediumship. The day and time of their services/evenings of mediumship are included with each organisations Name, address, Facebook link and website link.

Organisations that have not re-opened but have maintained a social media presence and/or had contact with myself to confirm the venue is re-opening have been included. However, where I have been unable to find a Facebook page or website and have no confirmation of the venue being open then they have not been included. This includes 14 Greater World Christian Spiritualist Churches (GW) and 13 Spiritualist National Union Churches (SNU).

Most of the organisations will hold healing sessions and/or open circles and closed development groups but these are not listed in this book but can be found on the organisations Facebook pages or Websites.

The organisations are grouped according to the broad area of the UK they are located.

There are additional organisations that only offer Spiritual Development Opportunities but these are not included in this book currently.

Angels' Blessing

Angels be around you,

In front of you and behind.

Protection circles tightly,

Keeping body safe and mind.

Angels be around you,

A blessing for you this day .

Angels' love surround you,

Walk in light, with love, we pray.

Veronica Jenkins

What is Spiritualism?

Spiritualism is a recognised religion within the UK with its roots at the dawn of the human journey. The ability to link with Spirits and "talk to the dead" is recorded across the world and is an integral part of ancient spiritual beliefs and practices with Mystics and seers having a key role in religious ceremonies and practices.

The religion of Spiritualism is formed around mediums providing evidence of survival of the spirit after the death of the physical body. The philosophical thinking of Spiritualism follows from the acceptance of the Spiritual world. This thinking is exemplified by recognising that our eternal Spirit is interconnected with the energy and Spirit of others. This interconnectedness is recognised by many as "God" and our Spirit emanating from this being the Fatherhood of God.

The following 7 Principles are tenets of faith of the Spiritualist National Union (SNU)

1, Fatherhood of God

2, Brotherhood of Man

3, The communion of Spirits and the Ministry of Angels

4, The continuous existence of the human soul

5, Personal responsibility

6, Compensation and retribution hereafter for all the good and evil deeds done on Earth

7, Eternal progress open to every human soul.

Christian Spiritualists have additional tenets around the role of Jesus in their faith.

What happens at a Spiritualist Service?

A Spiritualist Service is at it's heart an expression of faith through prayers, songs, readings, spiritual philosophy, reflection, healing and proof of survival of Spirit through the mediumship of guest speakers.

The mediumship element of a service is where the medium will link with Spirits connected to people in the congregation. These can be loved ones, family, neighbours, work colleagues, friends or pets. The mediums will communicate the emotions, memories, character and physical attributes of the loved one, often they are able to communicate additional information such as names, dates, addresses and events that are happening in a member of congregations' life. Sometimes a medium knows who the information they are giving is for within the congregation, other times they give the information to the congregation as a whole and wait for someone to indicate that they can take the information as relevant to someone they know in Spirit.

A service or evening of mediumship will have as a minimum an opening prayer, mediumship and a closing prayer. Venues often charge entry for these events.

A Divine Service will include, in addition to the above service elements, readings, songs/music, healing and spiritual philosophy. Divine Services are usually free to enter but a collection is taken during or after the service.

Raffles are usually held to raise funds for the organisation and help pay for building costs and mediums expenses. Raffle prizes are always welcome.

Traditionally refreshments have been available at venues after services but COVID has meant some venues no longer offer this service.

You do not have to be a "believer" to come to our services but please come with an open mind and a respect for the other people attending.

Many people first come to our services seeking reassurance about a loved one who has passed to Spirit and this is an important role of our organisations. However, there is no guaranteed that a medium will link with the loved one you are seeking or come to you with any message at all. In services mediums do not choose who comes through, as they usually allow Spirit to prioritise communications. Additionally, as it is a public meeting, mediums and Spirit themselves are sensitive to overwhelming grief that can accompany communication with someone recently passed.

Many venues offer weekly healing from trained healers, open circles and development groups.

Workshops on specific areas of Spiritualism are sometimes available through the year as are Psychic Suppers.

Many venues offer private mediumship readings, please ask about details of what is available after a service, if interested.

Special events are sometimes held at a premium price by venues. These events are usually longer than services and are focused on mediumship.

Venues usually open about 30 minutes before the start of a meeting. Please arrive between 5 and 10 minutes before the start of a service so you don't disrupt the meeting which usually begin promptly.

If you have any questions following a service then please seek the advice of a member of the organisations committee or the person who chaired the meeting.

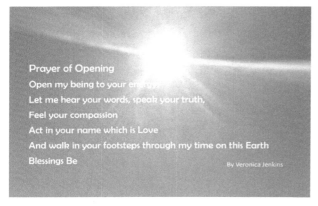

Prayer of Opening

Open my being to your energy

Let me hear your words, speak your truth,

Feel your compassion

Act in your name which is Love

And walk in your footsteps through my time on this Earth

Blessings Be

By Veronica Jenkins

Impact of COVID

No book would be complete at the current time without mentioning COVID. COVID has hit many Spiritualist organisations over the last two years either through the loss of church members to the virus or due to the prolonged lockdowns impacting the finances of organisations. As a consequence, there have been several venues closed due to finances and/or Churches not being able to form a committee to run the organisation.

Most organisations have now re-opened, however, with the recent Omicrom variant, some have extended their Christmas close down period into February. Many of the open venues have reduced the number or frequency of services to what happened before lockdown. A small number of churches have not re-opened from the last lockdown but are still active on Facebook and hoping to re-open.

It is advisable to check the Facebook page or website of an organisation before attending for the first time to ensure that the service is on and their current requirements with regard to COVID i.e. facemasks or test results.

I would like to take this opportunity to give my heartfelt thanks to the churches and organisations who have maintained their spiritual services online throughout lockdown. They have been a lifeline to many and brought our religion to a new audience across the world.

My special thanks to the following who provided these services through lockdown: Amadeity, Spiritual Psychics TV (SPtv), Totton Spiritualist Church, Wimbledon Spiritualist Church, Blue Lodge Droitwich Spiritual Centre, Carterton Spiritualist Church, Lechlade Spiritualist Church, Victoria Road Spiritualist Church, Clitheroe Spiritualist Church, Poole Christian Spiritualist Church, New Addington Spiritual and Healing Centre (NASH), Norton Christian Spiritualist Church, Stockton Spiritualist Church, Arthur Conan Doyle Centre, Spiritualist Association of Great Britain (SAGB)

If love was enough to heal you

If love was enough to heal you,
You would be safe and well this day.

If love was enough to heal you,
You would never be sick, not one day.

If love was enough to save you,
You would live in my arms every day.

But you have your own journey to travel,
Your own lessons and experiences to give.

You have your own journey to travel,
A pathway that's not mine to live.

I give you my love not to change you,
But to enable your lessons to be learnt.

I give you my love not to keep you,
But to set you free to your Spirit, my love.

Veronica Jenkins

Definition of Geographical Area

To make finding local churches easier in this book I have divided England into a number of Areas:

East Midlands - Lincolnshire, Derbyshire, Nottinghamshire, Leicestershire, Northamptonshire

Eastern - Norfolk and Suffolk

London - All areas within the M25

North East - Durham, Northumberland

North West - Cheshire, Lancashire and Cumbria

South East - The area south of Suffolk, Northamptonshire and Cambridgeshire, east of the A34 from Oxford downwards, minus the area within the M25

South West - The area south of Herefordshire, Worcestershire and Warwickshire, west of the A34 from Oxford downwards

West Midlands - Staffordshire, Warwickshire, Shropshire and Herefordshire

Yorkshire - The County of Yorkshire

East Midlands

Bedford Spiritualist Church (SNU)

Services on: Thursdays at 19:30; Sundays at 18:00

21 Ashburnham Road, Bedford MK40 1DX

https://www.facebook.com/Bedford-Spiritualist-Church-288537244546058

Beeston Spiritualist Group

Services on: Sundays at 18:00

Chilwell Memorial Hall, 129 High Rd, Beeston, Nottingham NG9 4AT

https://www.facebook.com/Beeston-Spiritualist-grp-103189412058615

Belper Spiritualist Church (SNU)

Services on: Mondays at 13:15

Jubilee Hall, 5 New Road, Belper DE56 1US

https://www.facebook.com/groups/1444127668963544

-

Bourne Spiritualist Centre

Services on: Saturdays at 18:30; 1st Wednesday of a month at 19:30

19A North Street, Bourne PE109AE

https://www.facebook.com/Bournespiritualistcentre

Bracebridge Heath Spiritualist Centre

Services on: Sundays at 19:15

The Pavillion, Bath Road, Bracebridge Heath, Lincoln LN4 2TU

https://www.facebook.com/groups/1466734253579112

-

Brimington & Calow Spiritualist Church

Services on: Sundays at 18:30

Calow Community Center, Allpits Road, Calow, Chesterfield S44 5AT

https://www.facebook.com/groups/222747521419871

-

Buxton Spiritualist Church (SNU)

Services on: Sundays at 18:30

2 Holker Road, Buxton SK176QN

https://www.facebook.com/Buxton-Spiritualist-Church-117745883432153

-

Chesterfield Spiritualist Centre (SNU)

Services on: Saturdays at 19:00

55-57 Baden Powell Road, Chesterfield S40 2SL

https://www.facebook.com/Chesterfield-Spiritualist-Centre-320595718067461

-

Clay Cross Spiritualist Church (SNU)

Services on: Sundays at 18:30

Bridge St, Clay Cross, Chesterfield S45 9NG

https://www.facebook.com/claycross.spchurch.3

-

Coalville Spiritualist Church (SNU)

Services on: Sundays at 18:00

54 Bridge Road, Coalville, Leicestershire LE67 3PW

https://www.facebook.com/Coalville-Spiritualist-Church-108205147737796

-

Darley Dale Christian Spiritualist Church

Services on: Sundays at 18:30

The Mencap Centre (in the grounds of Darley Dale Primary School), Greenaway Lane, Hackney, Matlock, DE4 2Q

https://www.facebook.com/Darley-Dale-CS-Church-175974433353393/

-

Derby Charnwood Spiritualist Church (SNU)

Services on: Mondays at 13:45; Sundays at 10:30

18 Charnwood Street, Derby DE1 2GY

https://www.facebook.com/derbycharnwood

-

Eastwood Spiritualist Centre (SNU)

Services on: Wednesdays at 19:00; Sundays at 11:00

Edward Road, Eastwood, Nottingham NG16 3EU

https://www.facebook.com/Eastwood-Spiritualist-Centre-366295550145447

When we define ourselves by our past we lose hope.

When we define ourselves with hope we create our future.

Edwinstowe Spiritualist Church

Services on: Sundays at 18:30

Edwinstowe Village Hall, Mansfield Road, Edwinstowe, Nottinghamshire NG21 9NJ

https://www.facebook.com/groups/170993919729397

-

Glossop Spiritualist Centre

Services on: Sundays at 19:30

The Commercial Inn function room, 137 Manor Park Road, Glossop SK13 7SH

https://www.facebook.com/glossopspiritualistcentre

-

Grimsby Spiritualist Church (SNU)

Services on: Sundays at 18:30

35-39 Duncombe Street, Grimsby, Humberside DN32 7SG

https://www.facebook.com/groups/267857594106051

-

Hadfield Spiritualist Church (SNU)

Services on: Thursdays at 19:45

7 Jones Street, Hadfield, High Peak, Derbyshire SK13 1BZ

https://www.facebook.com/hadfieldspiritualist

THE MYSTIC MOON

The Mystic Moon
29 Hall Street, Sherwood, Nottingham,
NG5 4AS

Heart & Soul Connections

Services on: Tuesdays at 19:30

Field Lane Community Centre, Field Lane, Alvaston, Derby, DE24 0GW

https://www.facebook.com/groups/186512021375489/

https://heartandsoulderby.wixsite.com/heartandsoulderby

-

Horninglow Spiritualist Church

Services on: Sundays at 10:00

Farm Road, Burton-on-Trent DE13 0XQ

https://www.facebook.com/groups/hornonglow

-

Kettering Spiritualist Church (SNU)

Services on: Sundays at 15:00

St. Peters Avenue, Kettering NN16 0HD

https://www.facebook.com/Kettering-Spiritualist-Church-282696175196703

-

Kirkby in Ashfield Spiritualist Church (SNU)

Services on: Mondays at 19:00; Sundays at 19:00

Lowmoor Road, Kirkby in Ashfield, Nottinghamshire NG17 7BH

https://www.facebook.com/groups/123838277722318

Leicester Progressive Spiritualist Teaching & Development Centre (SNU)

Services on: Mondays at 19:30; Wednesdays at 14:30; Sundays at 18:00

4 St James Street, Lee Circle, Leicester LE1 3SU

https://www.facebook.com/leicesterprogressive

http://www.progressivespiritualistchurch.co.uk/

-

Long Eaton Spiritualist Church (SNU)

Services on: Sundays at 18:30

Broad Street, Long Eaton, Nottingham NG10 1LF

https://www.facebook.com/Long-Eaton-Spiritualist-Church-Broad-Street-339327086117244

-

Loughborough Spiritualist Church (SNU)

Services on: Tuesdays at 19:30; Sundays at 15:00

Steeple Row, Loughborough, Leicestershire LE11 1UX

https://www.facebook.com/Loughborough-SNU-Spiritualist-Church-101209145468480

-

Mansfield Spiritualist Centre (SNU)

Services on: Wednesdays at 19:30; Sundays at 18:30

Dallas Street, Mansfield NG18 5SZ

https://www.facebook.com/mansfieldspiritualistcentre

Northampton Spiritualist Church (SNU)

Services on: Sundays at 18:30

89 St Michael's Road, Northampton, NN1 3JT

https://www.facebook.com/groups/251915571516192

https://northamptonspiritualists.org/

-

Nottingham First Spiritualist Church (SNU)

Services on: Saturdays at 19:00; Sundays at 18:30

Rise Park Community Centre, Bestwood Park Drive West, Nottingham NG5 5EJ

https://www.facebook.com/nottinghamfirstspiritualistchurch

Nottingham Spiritualist Church Hall Street (SNU)

Services on: Mondays at 14:00; Sundays at 18:30

Hall Street, Sherwood, Nottingham NG5 4AS

https://www.facebook.com/nottinghamspiritualists

https://www.nottinghamspiritualistchurch.com/

Retford Spiritualist Society

Services on: not open at the moment

40 Chapelgate, St Stephens House, Chapelgate, Retford DN22 6PJ

https://www.facebook.com/retford.soceity/

Ripley Spiritualist Church (SNU)

Services on: Sundays at 18:00

26-28 Grosvenor Road, Ripley, Derbyshire DE5 3JF

https://www.facebook.com/DerbyshireSNU

-

Rushden Independent Spiritualist Church

Services on: Sundays at 15:00

1a Moor Road Rushden Northamptonshire NN10 9SP

https://www.facebook.com/groups/522298405181118

-

Sleaford Spiritualist Church (SNU)

Services on: Sundays at 18:30

100 Westgate, Sleaford, Lincs NG34 7WN

https://www.facebook.com/Sleaford-Spiritualist-Centre-186436631479084

-

South Nottinghamshire Spiritualist Church

Services on: Tuesdays at 19:30; Fridays at 13:30; Saturdays at 19:30

Wilford and South Notts Community Centre, Wilford Lane, Nottingham NG11 7AX

https://www.facebook.com/West-Bridgford-Spiritualist-church-284892999618

-

Spirit Links Derby

Services on: Fridays at 7pm

Shelton Lock Community Welfare Centre, Chellaston Road, Derby DE24 9EF

https://www.facebook.com/groups/1576382129257884/

Spirit Tree

Services on: Tuesdays at 19:00

The Beaumont Centre, Nottingham Road, Coleorton, Leicester LE67 8HN

https://www.facebook.com/groups/586650864729082

-

Staveley Spiritual Group

Services on: Sundays at 18:30

The Hollingwood in Hollingwood, Pine Street, Hollingwood, Chesterfield S43 2LG

https://www.facebook.com/groups/1707261882875906

-

Sutton In Ashfield Spiritualist Church "The Twitchell" (SNU)

Services on: Mondays at 19:00; Sundays at 18:15

35 The Twitchell, Sutton-in-Ashfield, Nottinghamshire NG17 5DF

https://www.facebook.com/SuttonInAshfieldSpiritualistChurchTheTwitchell

-

Swadlincote Spiritualist Church

Services on: Wednesdays at 19:15; Sundays at 18:00

Highfield Street, Swadlincote, DE11 9AS

https://www.facebook.com/groups/294217478079

The Lighthouse Bingham Spiritualist Church

Services on: Sundays at 18:30

Long Acre Studios, 26 Long Acre, Bingham, NG13 8BG

https://www.facebook.com/The-Lighthouse-Bingham-Spiritualist-Church-744241872424282

-

The Spiritual Light Centre

Services on: 2nd Sunday of each month at 18:30

Framework Knitters Museum Chapel, Chapel Street, Ruddington. NG11 6HE

https://www.facebook.com/spirituallightruddington

-

Wellingborough Christian Spiritualist Church

Services on: Thursdays at 19:30

The Quaker Meeting House, St Johns Street, Wellingborough NN8 4LG

https://www.facebook.com/wellingboroughchristianspritualistchurch/

https://www.wellingboroughchristianspiritualistchurch.com/

-

Worksop Spiritualist Church (SNU)

Services on: Saturdays at 19:00; Sundays at 18:30

37 George Street, Worksop S80 1QJ

https://www.facebook.com/groups/198112932338698

Yataheeh

Services on: online only at the moment

641 Melton Road, Leicester LE4 8EB

https://www.facebook.com/yataheehs

A Feather Drifted Down

A feather drifted down,

Close by me, today.

I smiled gently crying,

Knowing Angels heard me pray.

A feather fell in front of me,

As I was thinking of you.

A sign from the Angels,

That you think of me too.

A feather rested before me,

As I opened the door,

I knew it was a sign,

You were there ever more.

Angels gift us feathers.

A symbol of peace.

Know they are here for you,

Bringing your loved ones and peace.

Veronica Jenkins

Eastern

Angel Voices Bradwell

Services on: Sundays at 19:00

2 Green Lane Bradwell, Great Yarmouth NR31 8QH

https://www.facebook.com/bradwellspiritualistchurch

-

Awareness Spiritual Centre

Services on: Wednesdays at 18:30

Barnhall Community and Social Club, Alderney Gardens, Wickford SS11 7JP

https://www.facebook.com/TheCrystalPyramidServices/

-

Boston Spiritual Reconnections

Services on: Sundays at 18:30

Rochford Tower Village Hall, Rochford Tower Lane, Boston PE21 9RQ

https://www.facebook.com/Boston-Spiritual-reconnections-182233025209684

-

Cambridge Spiritual Centre (ISM)

Services on: Monthly meetings

Harston Village Hall, 20 High Street, Harston, Cambridge CB22 7PX

https://www.facebook.com/Institute-of-Spiritualist-Mediums-CambridgeUK-222671873041328/

Dereham Spiritualist Church

Services on: Sundays at 18:30

Wix's Yard, off the High Street, Dereham NR19 1DR

https://www.facebook.com/DerehamIndependentSpiritualistChurch

-

Ely and District Spiritualist Church (SNU)

Services on: Wednesdays at 19:30

The Ely Museum/The Old Gaol, Market Street, Ely CB7 4LS

https://www.facebook.com/groups/158976537488629

-

Godmanchester Spiritualist Church

Services on: 1st Sunday of a month at 18:00

Rose and Crown Quaker Centre, 48 Post St, Godmanchester, Huntingdon, PE29 2AQ

https://www.facebook.com/PE292AQ

-

Guardian Angels Spiritual Church

Services on: Thursdays at 18:00

Northborough Village Hall, Cromwell Close, Northborough PE6 9DP

https://www.facebook.com/guardianangelsspirit/

-

Harbour Lights Spiritual Group

Services on: Sundays at 19:00

Council Hall, Yarmouth Road, Caister NR30 5DL

https://www.facebook.com/caistercouncilhall

Hopton Spiritualist Centre (SNU)

Services on: Sundays at 15:00

Village Hall, Station Road, Hopton, Great Yarmouth NR31 9BE

https://www.facebook.com/Hopton-Spiritualist-and-Healing-Center-102208063191942

-

Little Acorn Spiritualist Centre

Services on: 1st Sunday of a month at 18:45

Long Meadows Community Centre, Harwich CO12 4US

https://www.facebook.com/LittleAcornCSC

-

Littleport Christian Spiritualists

Services on: Thursdays at 19:40

Littleport Village Hall, Victoria Street, Littleport, Cambs CB6 1LX

https://www.facebook.com/Rev.Nick.Brown/

-

Lowestoft Spiritualist Church (SNU)

Services on: Sundays at 18:30

13 Gordan Road, Lowestoft, Suffolk NR32 1NL

https://www.facebook.com/groups/547899751921147

-

Mighty Oaks and Sunflowers Centre

Services on: 2nd Friday of a month at 19:30

Ivo Day Centre, Albion Street, Spalding PE11 2AU

https://www.facebook.com/groups/121777107933906

Newmarket Pioneer Centre (SNU)

Services on: 1st Friday of a month at 19:30; Sundays at 11:00

The Scout Hut, Cardigan Street, Newmarket CB8 8HZ

https://www.facebook.com/Newmarket.Pioneers/

https://newmarketsnupioneercentre.org/

-

Norfolk Spiritualist Centre

Services on: Alternate Tuesdays at 19:30

Roxley Hall, 66 Yarmouth Road, Norwich NR7 0QF

https://www.facebook.com/groups/1401956923445048

-

Norwich Spiritualist Church (SNU)

Services on: Sundays at 18:30

Chapel Field North, Norwich, Norfolk NR2 1NY

https://www.facebook.com/groups/356266841076799

-

Rae of Light Events

Services on: Monthly events

The Queens Hall, Norwich Road, Watton IP25 6DA

https://www.facebook.com/raeoflightevents

-

Sacred Souls

Services on: Tuesdays at 19:30

Prickwillow Village Hall, Main Road, Prickwillow, Ely, Cambridgeshire CB7 4UN

https://www.facebook.com/groups/172668816428060/

Silver Cord

Services on: Sundays at 19:00

Oulton Community Centre, Meadow Drive, Oulton, Lowestoft NR32 3AZ

https://www.facebook.com/Silver-Cord-110689247062300

-

Snettisham Spiritualist Church

Services on: Alternate Sundays at 15:30

Memorial Hall, Old Church Road, (Next to the Rose and Crown), Snettisham, Norfolk PE31 7NA

https://www.facebook.com/groups/257198444728398/

-

Spiritual Wings Spiritual Centre Holbeach

Services on: Alternate Tuesdays at 19:30

W.I. Hall, Park Road, Holbeach PE12 7EE

https://www.facebook.com/groups/1780565458831917

-

St Ives Spiritualist Church

Services on: Monthly on a Saturday at 19:30; Sundays at 18:30

Free Church Passage, Off Market Hill, St Ives, Cambridgeshire PE27 5AY

https://www.facebook.com/St-Ives-Spiritualist-Church-1627856650621129/

https://stivesspiritualistchurch.co.uk/

Swaffham Spiritual Awareness Group

Services on: Sundays at 18:30

Community Centre, Campinglands, Swaffham PE37 7RD

https://www.facebook.com/swaffham-spiritual-awareness-group-ssag-239996248748

-

Transformation Spiritual Centre

Services on: Thursdays at 19:30

Hemswell/Harpswell Hall, Maypole Street, Hemswell Village, Gainsborough, Lincs DN21 5UL

https://www.facebook.com/groups/341552449364830

-

Weeley Spiritualist Centre

Services on: 2nd and 4th Wednesday at 19:30

Weeley Village Hall, Clacton Road, Weeley, Weeley Heath, Clacton-on-Sea CO16 9DH

https://www.facebook.com/groups/154109791429260

-

Whispering Light Spiritual Group

Services on: Sundays at 19:00

Telecom Social Club, 18 Clapham Road Lowestoft NR32 1QR

https://www.facebook.com/groups/474136592656115

Wisbech Christian Spiritualist Church

Services on: Sundays at 15:00

Alexandra Road, Wisbech PE13 1HG

https://www.facebook.com/groups/103545889695382

-

Witham Spiritual Centre (ISM)

Services on: monthly meetings

The Labour Hall, Collingwood Road, (Opp. Station) Witham CM8 2EE

https://www.facebook.com/instituteofspiritualistmediums

The Song of Listening

Have you listened to the wind?
Have you listened to the birds?
Have you listened to the calm of nature?

Have you listened to the silence?
Have you listened to the night?
Have you listened to the peace that is being?

Have you listened to your heart?
Have you listened to your soul?
Have you listened to your God, He is speaking!

He is speaking of love,
He is speaking of peace,
He is speaking of the meaning of giving.

Listen with your heart,
Listen with your soul,
Listen with the whole of your being.

The voice that is God,
The voice that is peace,
Is gently waiting for you to listen.

Veronica Jenkins 2020

London

Acton Spiritual Centre (SNU)

Services on: Wednesdays at 19:00

"The Cottage", Woodhurst Road, Acton, London W3 6SL

https://www.facebook.com/actonspiritualcentre

-

Angels of Light Spiritual Sanctuary

Services on: Thursdays at 19:30

Tredegar Community Centre, 333 Morville Street, London E3 2DZ

https://www.facebook.com/angelsoflight.E3

-

Balham Spiritualist Church (SNU)

Services on: Sundays at 11:00

211A Balham High Road, London SW17 7BQ

https://www.facebook.com/Balhamspiritualistchurch

-

Barnes Healing Church

Services on: Sundays at 18:30

77 – 79 White Hart Lane, Barnes, London SW13 0QA

https://www.facebook.com/barneshealingchurch

http://barneshealingchurch.co.uk/

Barnet Christian Spiritualist Church

Services on: Sundays at 18:30

Union Street, Barnet, London EN5 4HY

https://www.facebook.com/BarnetCSC

-

Beacon of Light Spiritualist Church Enfield (SNU)

Services on: Sundays at 18:30

331 Carterhatch Lane, Enfield EN1 4AW

https://www.facebook.com/beacononoflightspiritualistchurchenfield

-

Bethnal Green Sanctuary of Spiritual Connections

Services on: Thursdays at 19:30

Cranbrook Community Centre, Mace Street, Bethnal Green, London E2 0RB

https://www.facebook.com/loveandlightE2/

-

Borehamwood Spiritual Centre

Services on: Thursdays at 20:00

Room 5, The Manor House, Allum Manor, Allum Lane, Borehamwood WD6 3PJ

https://www.facebook.com/BhwSpiritual

Bushey Spiritual Harmony Centre

Services on: 1st and 3rd Monday of the month at 19:30

The Bushey Arena, London Road, Bushey, London WD23 3AA

https://www.facebook.com/Bushey-Spiritual-Harmony-Centre-462421757271774

-

Canvey Spiritualist Church

Services on: Sundays at 18:30

57 Point Road, Canvey Island, Essex SS8 7TT

https://www.facebook.com/groups/567159100039970

-

Chelmsford Spiritualist Society

Services on: Wednesdays at 19:30; Sundays at 18:30

10 South Primrose Hill, Chelmsford CM1 2RG

https://www.facebook.com/Chelmsford-Spiritualist-Society-337896408101/

-

Clapham Spiritualist Church (SNU)

Services on: Saturdays at 19:30; Sundays at 18:00

11a North Street, Old Town, Clapham, London SW4 0HN

https://www.facebook.com/Clapham-Spiritualist-Church-130796680901559/

-

Colchester Spiritualist Church (SNU)

Services on: Thursdays at 19:30

Fennings Chase, off Priory Street, Colchester, Essex CO1 2QG

https://www.facebook.com/ColchesterSpiritualistCentre

Croydon Spiritualist Church (SNU)

Services on: Sundays at 11:00; Wednesdays at 19:45

Chatsworth Road, Croydon CR0 1HE

https://www.facebook.com/www.croydonspiritualistchurch.org.uk

-

Ealing National Spiritualist Church (SNU)

Services on: Thursdays at 19:30; Sundays at 18:30

66-68 Uxbridge Road, Ealing, London W13 8RA

https://www.facebook.com/ealingnationalspiritualistchurch/

-

Eltham Spiritualist Church (SNU)

Services on: Sundays at 18:30

64a Well Hall Road, Eltham, London SE9 6SH

https://www.facebook.com/elthamspiritualchurch

https://sites.google.com/site/elthamspiritualistchurch

-

Forget-me-not Sanctuary of Spiritual Friends

Services on: Tuesdays at 20:00

St Mary's community Centre, 180 Eltham High Street, Eltham, London SE9 1BJ

https://www.facebook.com/Forget-me-not-sanctuary-of-spiritual-friends-1465713607019159

-

Fulham Spiritualist Church (SNU)

Services on: Sundays at 18:30

Kelvedon Road , Fulham, London SW6 5BP

https://www.facebook.com/fulhamspiritualist.church

-

Garston Spiritualist Church

Services on: Sundays at 18:30

First Avenue, Watford WD25 9PS

https://www.facebook.com/garstonspiritualist.church

-

Grays Spiritualist Church

Services on: Wednesdays at 14:00; Sundays at 18:00

168 Rectory Road, Grays RM17 5SJ

https://www.facebook.com/grays.centre

-

Hampton Hill Spiritualist Church (SNU)

Services on: Thursdays at 19:30; Sundays at 18:30

Angel Close, Hampton Hill, Hampton, London TW12 1RG

https://www.facebook.com/groups/250236938966969

-

Harrow Spiritualist Church (SNU)

Services on: Wednesdays at 19:30

1 Vaughan Road, Harrow, Middlesex HA1 4DP

https://www.facebook.com/groups/770248850261353

https://harrowsnuchurch.wixsite.com/harrow

Hayes Spiritualist Church (SNU)

Services on: monthly zoom meetings currently

Albert Hall, Albert Road, Hayes, Middlesex UB3 4HR

https://www.facebook.com/HayesChurch

-

Hinton Road Spiritual Church Uxbridge 'House of the Good Shepherd'

Services on: Tuesdays at 14:00; Sundays at 18:30

HintonRoad, Uxbridge UB8 2DL

https://www.facebook.com/groups/113966178614763

-

Hounslow Spiritualist Centre (SNU)

Services on: Once a month on a Wednesday at 19:30

14/15 Hanworth Terrace, Hounslow, Middlesex TW3 3TS

https://www.facebook.com/Hounslow-Spiritualist-CentreChurch-356798714518723

https://hounslowspiritualistcentre.co.uk

-

Ilford Spiritualist Church (SNU)

Services on: Thursdays at 13:30

370 – 372 High Road, Ilford IG1 1QP

https://www.facebook.com/Ilford-Spiritualist-Church-137068806658360

-

Independent Spiritual Group

Services on: Sundays at 18:30

Orpington Liberal Club Hall, 7 Station Road, Orpington BR6 0RZ

https://www.facebook.com/independantspiritualgroup

https://www.independantspiritualgroup.uk

-

Jennings Street Christian Spiritualist Church

Services on: Sundays at 18:30

Jennings Street, Swindon Village, London SN2 2BG

https://www.facebook.com/Christian-spiritualist-church-Jennings-Street-112407127885798

-

Kingston National Spiritualist Church (SNU)

Services on: Mondays at 19:30; Sundays at 11:00

Villiers Road, Kingston-upon-Thames, Surrey, KT1 3AR

https://www.facebook.com/KingstonNSC

https://kingstonsc.net/

-

Letchworth Spiritualist Church (SNU)

Services on: 1st Sunday of a month at 18:30

Howard Garden Social Centre, Norton Way South, Letchworth Garden City, Hertfordshire

https://www.facebook.com/groups/letchworthspiritualistchurch1

-

Little Ilford National Spiritualist Church (SNU)

Services on: Wednesdays at 19:30; Sundays at 18:30

111 Third Avenue, Manor Park, London E12 6DS

https://www.facebook.com/groups/1523760077692625

-

London Spiritual Mission

Services on: Wednesdays at 19:30; Sundays at 18:30

13 Pembridge Place, London W2 4XB

https://www.facebook.com/spiritualmission

https://spiritualmission.co.uk/

-

Manor Park Spiritualist Church (SNU)

Services on: Sundays at 18:30

145 Shrewsberry Road, Forest Gate, Manor Park, London E7 8QA

https://www.facebook.com/groups/314770955240127

-

North London Spiritualist Church (SNU)

Services on: Wednesdays at 19:30; Saturdays at 19:30

425 Hornsey Road, London N19 4DX

http://www.nlsc.org.uk/

-

Queensway Spiritual Centre

Services on: Sundays at 18:30

1st Hemel Hempstead Scouts HQ Queensway, Hemel Hempstead HP2 5DF

https://www.facebook.com/Queensway-Spiritual-Centre-444058648971946

Richmond Spiritualist Church (SNU)

Services on: Wednesdays at 19:30; Sundays at 18:30

97 Church Road, Richmond, Surrey, London TW10 6LU

https://www.facebook.com/richmondspiritualistchurch

-

Romford Spiritualist Centre (ISM)

Services on: 2nd Tuesday of each month at 19:30

Cranham Social Club. 103 Front Lane, Upmister, Essex RM14 1XN

https://www.facebook.com/ISMRomford

http://www.ism.org.uk/ism-branches/romford-branch

-

Southall Spiritualist Church (SNU)

Services on: Thursdays at 19:30; Sundays at 19:00

Hortus Road, The Green, Southall, Middlesex UB2 4AL

https://www.facebook.com/groups/SouthallSpiritualist

http://www.southallspiritualists.webeden.co.uk/

-

Spiritualist Association of Great Britain - various

Services on: various please check with website

341 Queenstown Road, Battersea, London SW8 4LH

https://www.facebook.com/SAGBORGUK

-

St Albans Spiritualist Church (SNU)

Services on: Thursdays at 19:30; Sundays at 18:30

40 Granville Road, St Albans, Hertfordshire, AL1 5BQ

https://www.facebook.com/stalbansspiritualistchurch1

-

Stockwell Spiritualist Church (SNU)

Services on: Fridays at 19:30; 3rd Sunday of a month at 18:30

St Michael Road, Stockwell, London SW9 0SL

https://www.facebook.com/Stockwell-Spiritualist-Church-306401836747975

-

Sutton Spiritualist Church (SNU)

Services on: Thursdays 19:45; Sundays 18:45

St Barnabas Road, Sutton SM1 4NP

https://www.facebook.com/suttonspiritualchurch

-

Sydenham Spiritual and Healing Centre

Services on: Wednesdays at 19:30

Venner Road Hall, Venner Road, Sydenham SE26 5EQ

https://www.facebook.com/www.sydenhamspiritualcentre.co.uk/

-

Temple of Light Christian Spiritualist Church Laindon

Services on: Sundays at 18:30

8 Bedford Road, Laidon, Basildon SS15 6PG

https://www.facebook.com/templeoflightspiritualistchurchlaindon/

-

The Haven in Grays

Services on: Sundays at 19:00

Belmont Hall, Parker Road, Grays RM17 5YN

https://www.facebook.com/groups/1029214854558941

-

The Lighthouse Spiritualist Centre

Services on: Tuesdays at 19:30

The South Norwood & Woodside Social Club, 12 Enmore Road, Croydon, London SE25 5NQ

https://www.facebook.com/groups/374205359421854

-

The Oakes Spiritualist Centre

Services on: Fridays at 19:30

Emerson Park Community Centre, Slewing Lane, Hornchurch RM11 2BU

https://www.facebook.com/The-Oakes-Spiritual-Page-135157607038256

-

Thundersley Christian Spiritualist Church

Services on: Sunday at 18:30

Coombe Wood, Bread & Cheese Hill, Thundersley, Essex SS7 1AW

https://www.facebook.com/TCSChurchUK

-

Wakering Spiritual Centre

Services on: Thursdays at 20:00

Memorial Hall, High Street, Great Wakering, Essex SS3 0EF

https://www.facebook.com/Wakering-Spiritual-Centre-126175137464283

Walthamstowe Vestry Road Spiritualist Church (SNU)

Services on: closed indefinitely due to work needing to be done on roof

Vestry Road, London E17 9NH

http://www.vestryrdspiritualistchurch.co.uk/

-

Walton Spiritualist Church (SNU)

Services on: Wednesdays at 19:30; Sundays at 18:30

Hersham Road, Walton-On-Thames KT12 1RW

https://www.facebook.com/groups/136250356572985

-

Watford Christian Spiritualist Church

Services on: Sundays at 18:30

125 Estcourt Road, Watford

https://www.facebook.com/groups/913558996263967

-

Wickham Lane Spiritualist Church (SNU)

Services on: Wednesdays at 19:30; Sundays at 18:30

95 Wickham Lane, London SE2 0XW

https://www.facebook.com/Wickham-Lane-spiritualist-Church-2019-2314446508796362

-

Wimbledon Spiritualist Church

Services on: Sundays at 11:00

136 Hartfield Rd, Wimbledon, London SW19 3TG

https://www.facebook.com/groups/3516152137

Woodford Spiritualist Church (SNU)

Services on: Mondays at 14:00; Sundays at 18:00

9 Grove Crescent, South Woodford, London E18 2JR

https://www.facebook.com/groups/495785217466752

http://www.woodfordchurch.com/

Healing Prayer

As I open up my heart, mind and spirit to that love that is called God may I accept that love into my life that I may use that love in healing.

I ask that the healing energy reaches the four corners of the Earth, to the places I will never hear of and the people I will never meet but whose need is so desperate at this time.

I ask that that love goes to the Leaders of the World that the decisions they make enable us to live in peace and heal the Earth.

Coming closer to home enable me to focus that healing energy on my friends, my neighbours, my loved ones and the people made known to me in need of that healing balm.

Never forgetting the needs of the animals we share our planet and with whom we our lives, I send my healing thoughts to them.

And finally, I accept that healing energy into my own being that through that healing energy, I am best able to support the needs of others.

Blessings Be   Veronica Jenkins

North East

Ashington and Bedlington Spiritualist Church (SNU)

Services on: Wednesdays at 19:00; Sundays at 18:30

276 Hawthorn Road, Ashington, Northumberland NE63 9AY

https://www.facebook.com/Ashington-and-Bedlington-SNU-Spiritualist-Church-1637273996507654/

-

Beacon of Light Spiritualist Church

Services on: Thursdays at 19:30

Cloughdene, Tantobie, Stanley DH9 9PN

https://www.facebook.com/Beacon-of-Light-Spiritualist-Church-448349052019210

-

Billingham Spiritualist Church (SNU)

Services on: Sundays at 18:30

Chapel Road, Billingham, Stockton-On-Tees TS23 1DX

https://www.facebook.com/New-Billingham-SNU-Church-102347091447156

Birtley Spiritualist Church (SNU)

Services on: Mondays at 19:30

1A Mitchell Street, Birtley DH3 1LS

https://www.facebook.com/Birtley-Spiritualist-Church-598691133569770

Blackhill Spiritualist Church (SNU)

Services on: Sundays at 18:00

Off Park Road, Blackhill, Consett, County Durham DH8 5SP

https://www.facebook.com/BlackhillSpiritualistChurch/

-

Bloxham Spiritual Centre

Services on: Thursdays at 19:30

King's Sutton Memorial Hall, Astrop Road, King's Sutton, Banbury OX17 3PG

https://www.facebook.com/groups/406873107374410/

-

Chester-Le-Street Spiritualist Church (SNU)

Services on: Fridays at 19:00, Sundays at 18:00

2 Ashley Terrace, Chester-Le-Street, Co Durham DH3 3E

https://www.facebook.com/chesterlestreetspiritualistchurch

-

Chichester Christian Spiritualist Church – South Shields

Services on: Sundays at 18:30

40 Chichester Rd, South Shields NE33 4AF

https://www.facebook.com/groups/2486145944969800

-

Craghead Spiritualist Church (SNU)

Services on: Wednesdays at 19:00; Sundays at 18:00

3 Front Street, Craghead, Stanley DH9 6DS

https://www.facebook.com/Craghead-Spiritualist-Church-1641688592728736

Cramlington Spiritualist Church (SNU)

Services on: Sundays at 18:00

Cramlington Village Community Centre, East Farm Terrace, Cramlington, Northumberland NE23 1DT

https://www.facebook.com/CramlingtonSNUSpiritualistChurch

-

Darlington Spiritualist Church (SNU)

Services on: Sundays at 18:30

Denmark Street, Darlington DL3 0LP

https://www.facebook.com/DSCAAC/

-

Durham Spiritualist Church (SNU)

Services on: Sundays at 18:00

2 John St, Durham DH1 4DE

https://www.facebook.com/DurhamSpiritualistChurch

-

Gateshead Consecration Spiritualist Church (SNU)

Services on: WednesdayS at 19:00

35 Gladstone Terrace West, Gateshead NE8 4EF

https://www.facebook.com/Gateshead-Consecration-Spiritualist-Church-457015234653395

Gateshead Eden Progressive Spiritualist Church (SNU)

Services on: Sundays at 18:30

Rectory Hall, off Rectory Place, Bensham, Gateshead NE8 1XN

https://www.facebook.com/Gatesheadedenprogressive

-

Heaton & Byker Spiritualist Church (SNU)

Services on: Mondays at 19:00; Sundays at 18:30

16-18 Tosson Terrace, Heaton, Newcastle upon Tyne NE6 5LX

https://www.facebook.com/Heaton-Byker-Spiritualist-Church-400381330387192

-

Horden Spiritualist Church (SNU)

Services on: Sundays at 18:00

Yoden Way, Horden, Peterlee SR8 4JD

https://www.facebook.com/groups/287069884833985/

-

Jarrow Spiritualist Church (SNU)

Services on: Wednesdays at 19:00

Monkton Road, Jarrow NE32 3AF

https://www.facebook.com/jarrowchurch/

-

Leadgate Spiritualist Group

Services on: Thursdays at 19:00

Leadgate Centre, off Durham Road, Consett DH8 7RJ

https://www.facebook.com/groups/134388240430199

Marton and Hemlington Spirit Meetings

Services on: not open at the moment

Marton Community Centre, Cypress Road, Marton-in-Cleveland, Middlesbrough TS7 8QG

https://www.facebook.com/Martonandhemlington

Monkwearmouth Spiritualist Church (SNU)

Services on: Sundays at 18:30

150a Newcastle Road, Sunderland, Tyne & Wear, SR5 1NA

https://www.facebook.com/groups/1256792721159762

Newcastle Spiritual Evidence Society (SNU)

Services on: Sundays at 18:30

11 Osborne Road, Jesmond, Newcastle upon Tyne NE2 2AE

https://www.facebook.com/NewcastleSpiritualEvidenceSociety

-

North Shields Spiritualist Church (SNU)

Services on: Sundays at 18:30

Balkwell Community Welfare Association, Heaton Terrace, North Shields NE29 7LY

https://www.facebook.com/northshields.spiritualistchurch

Norton Christian Spiritualist Church

Services on: Sundays at 18:30

Darlington Lane, Stockton-on-Tees TS20 1ER

https://www.facebook.com/NortonCSC

https://norton-christian-spiritualist-church.webs.com/

Pegswood Spiritualist Church

Service on: Thursdays at 19:00

Union Building, Front Street, Pegswood NE61 6RG

https://www.facebook.com/groups/576330165752058

-

Philadelphia Spiritualist Church (SNU)

Services on: Sundays at 18:30

Chapel Row, Houghton-Le-Spring, DH4 4JD

https://www.facebook.com/Philadelphia-SNU-Spiritualist-Church-UK-174274906305595/

-

Saltburn Spiritualist Church (SNU)

Services on: not open at the moment

Coach House, Albion Terrace, Saltburn-by-the-Sea TS12 1JW

https://www.facebook.com/saltburnspiritualistchurch

-

Seaham Spiritualist Church (SNU)

Services on: Alternate Tuesdays at 19:00; Sundays at 18:30

Vane Hall, Cornelia Terrace, Seaham, SR7 7RY

https://www.facebook.com/groups/383644181082

Seaton Delaval Spiritualist Church (SNU)

Services on: Sundays at 18:30

Station Road, Seaton Delaval, Whitley Bay NE25 0PT

https://www.facebook.com/groups/seatondelavalspiritualistchurch/

-

Shildon Spiritualist Church (SNU)

Services on: Mondays at 19:00

Middleton Road, Shildon DL4 1NN

https://www.facebook.com/shildonsnu

-

Spennymoor Spiritualist Church (SNU)

Services on: Sundays at 18:00

Barnfield Road (behind WI house), Spennymoor DL16 6EB

https://www.facebook.com/SpennymoorSpiritualistChurch

-

Spiritualist Friendship Centre

Services on: Sundays at 18:00

Sixth Street, Horden SR8 4SE

https://www.facebook.com/spiritualistfriendshipcentre

-

Stockton Spiritual & Holistic Healing Centre - Elmwood

Services on: various please check with FB

Grangefield Community Centre, 195 Oxbridge Lane, Stockton-on-Tees TS18 4HY

and

Elmwood Youth and Community Centre, 53 Darlington Road, Stockton-On-Tees TS18 5EP

https://www.facebook.com/stocktonholistichealingcentre

-

Sunderland Spiritualist Church (SNU)

Services on: Tuesdays at 19:00; Sundays at 18:30

1 Grange Terrace, Sunderland SR2 7DG

https://www.facebook.com/Sunderland-Spiritualist-Church-1446778705567424

-

Wallsend Spiritualist Church (SNU)

Services on: Tuesdays at 19:00; Sundays at 18:30

182 Park Road, Wallsend, Newcastle NE28 7QS

https://www.facebook.com/groups/1425370511065640

-

Widdrington Spiritualist Church

Services on: Sundays at 18:00

Grange Road, Widdrington Station, Morpeth NE61 5LZ

no FB or website

-

Willington Spiritualist Church (SNU)

Services on: Sundays at 18:00

Chapel Street, Willington, Co Durham DL15 0EQ

https://www.facebook.com/willingtonsnu.church

A Prayer to Our Angels

Through good times and bad,
May Angels be with us.
When life is hollow and company scarce,
May Angels sit with us.
When we feel full of joy and life is light,
May Angels smile with us.
When the world feels flat and emotions down,
May Angels lift us up.
When things work out and achievements come,
May Angels accept our thanks.
When thoughts come too fast and anxiety cripples,
May Angels calm us down.
When a stranger smiles and gifts are given,
May Angels receive joy too.
When we feel trapped and stuck in one place,
May Angels guide our steps.
When we are able to support and give help others,
May Angels feel our compassion.
When decisions are too complex and too hard to make,
May Angels guide our thoughts.
When we feel the love of others and our hearts are full,
May Angels share that love.
When life is too hard and choices too heavy,
May Angels lighten our load.
When we give of ourselves and sacrifice for others,
May Angels reward us in heaven.
When hearts are broken and pain is too deep,
May Angels hold us in their arms.
When we send up our prayers and give out our healing,
May Angels join our thoughts.
When it is time for our bodies end and ultimate passing,
May Angels stay with us.
Angels, I pray, be around me.
Angels, I pray, protect me.
Angels, I pray, guide me.
Angels, I pray, live with me.
Blessings Be

Veronica Jenkins

North West

Altrincham Spiritualist Church (SNU)

Services on: Sundays at 11:30; Wednesdays at 19:30

Claredon Avenue, Altrincham, WA15 8HD

https://www.facebook.com/AltrinchamSpiritualistChurch

-

Aquarius Christian Spiritualist Church

Services on: Tuesdays at 19:30

Bury Spiritual Centre, Russell Street, Bury BL9 5AX

https://www.facebook.com/groups/495271170623574

-

Ashton Spiritualist Church (SNU)

Services on: Wednesdays at 19:30: Sundays at 15:00

Burlington Street/Progress Street, Ashton-Under-Lyne OL6 7HJ

https://www.facebook.com/Ashton-Spiritualist-Church-1903597346552754

-

Atlantis Mind Body Spirit and Holistic Therapies

Services on: Thursdays at 19:30

Heady Hill Community Centre, Whalley Road, Heywood OL10 3JG

https://www.facebook.com/reikistar

Bankfoot Spirirtualist Church (SNU)

Services on: Saturdays at 19:00

455 Bowling Old Lane, Bradford BD5 8HL

https://www.facebook.com/groups/55260881865

-

Birkenhead Spiritualist Church (SNU)

Services on: Sundays at 18:30

2 Mount Grove, Oxton, Birkenhead, Wirral, Merseyside CH41 2UJ

https://www.facebook.com/Birkenhead-SNU-Spiritualist-Church-152904868744187

-

Blackburn Spiritualist Centre (SNU)

Services on: Thursdays at 19:00; Sundays at 18:30

Princes Street, Blackburn BB2 1LS

https://www.facebook.com/BlackburnSpiritualistsCentre

-

Blackpool Albert Road Spiritualist Church (SNU)

Services on: Thursdays at 19:30

71 Albert Road, Blackpool, FY1 4PW

https://www.facebook.com/albert.road.543

-

Bolton Spiritualist Church (SNU)

Services on: Mondays at 14:00; Thursdays at 19:30

21 Bradford Street, Bolton BL2 1HT

https://www.facebook.com/Bolton-SNU-Church-The-Voice-351341225269795/

Bulk Road Spiritualist Church (SNU)

Services on: 2nd and 4th Sunday of each month at 18:30

7-11 Bulk Road, Lancaster LA1 1FD

https://www.facebook.com/groups/861339910566228

-

Burnley Spiritualist Church

Services on: Tuesdays at 19:30; Sundays at 15:00

Stanley Street, Burnley BB11 2HH

https://www.facebook.com/BurnleySpiritualistChurch

-

Bury Spiritual Centre (SNU)

Services on: Tuesdays at 19:30; Thursdays at 19:30

3 Russell Street, Bury, BL9 5AX

https://www.facebook.com/Bury-Spiritual-Centre-1756218367936847

-

Chester Spiritualist Church (SNU)

Services on: Wednesdays at 19:00; Sundays at 18:30

Common Hall Street, Chester CH1 2BJ

https://www.facebook.com/Chester-Spiritualist-Church-518760828616451

-

Cleveleys Spiritualist Church (SNU)

Services on: Mondays at 19:30; Wednesdays at 14:30; Sundays at 14:30

93 Beach Road, Thornton-Cleveleys FY5 1EW

https://www.facebook.com/CleveleysSpiritualistChurch

Clitheroe Spiritualist Church (SNU)

Services on: Tuesdays at 19:30; Sundays at 19:00

Greenacre Street, Clitheroe BB7 1ED

https://www.facebook.com/Clitheroe-Spiritualist-Church-Ribble-Valley-108895257471597

Colne Spiritualist Church (SNU)

Services on: Sundays at 18:30

59 Spring Lane, Colne, Lancashire BB8 9BD

https://www.facebook.com/colnesnuchurch

http://colnespiritualistchurch.co.uk/

-

Congleton Spiritualist Church (SNU)

Services on: Sundays at 18:00

15 Park Road, Congleton, CW12 1DS

https://www.facebook.com/CongletonSpiritualistChurch

-

Connections of Light Spiritualist Church (COL)

Services on: Wednesdays at 19:30

Chapels, Darwen BB3 0EE

https://www.facebook.com/connectionsoflight

-

Crewe Spiritualist Church (SNU)

Services on: Sundays at 18:30

4-8 Adelaide Street, Crewe CW1 3DT

https://www.facebook.com/CreweSpiritualistChurch

Dearnley Spiritual Society (SNU)

Services on: Thursdays at 19:30

14-16 New Road, Littleborough OL15 8LX

https://www.facebook.com/DearnleySpiritualSociety/

-

Denton Central Spiritualist Church (SNU)

Services on: Tuesdays at 19:30; Saturday at 19:30; Sundays at 15:00

Annan Street, Denton, Manchester M34 3FX

https://www.facebook.com/DentonSpiritualistChurch

-

Farnworth Christian Spiritualist Church

Services on: Wednesdays at 19:30; Saturdays at 19:30pm; Sundays at 18:30

11A Peel Street, Farnworth, Bolton BL4 8AA

https://www.facebook.com/groups/35112175985

-

Fleetwood Spiritualist Church (SNU)

Services on: Tuesdays at 19:30; Sundays at 18:30

5 Oak Street, Fleetwood FY7 6TN

https://www.facebook.com/fwoodsnuchurch

-

Furness Spiritualist Church

Services on: Sundays at 18:30

Dalton Community Centre, Nelson Street, Dalton in Furness LA15 8AF

https://www.facebook.com/furnessspiritualistchurch

Great Harwood Spiritualist Church (SNU)

Services on: Saturdays at 19:00; alternate Wednesdays at 19:30

Clayton Street, Great Harwood, Lancashire BB6 7AQ

https://www.facebook.com/groups/240700503132186

-

Harley Street Spiritualist Church

Services on: Sundays at 18:30

Harley Street, Barrow in Furness LA14 1HS

https://www.facebook.com/harleystreetspiritualist

-

Heavens Gateway Spiritual Centre

Services on: Tuesdays at 19:15

The Clifton Centre, 6 Wynne Avenue, Clifton, Manchester M27 8FU

https://www.facebook.com/groups/2022538654673778

-

Horwich National Spiritualist Church (SNU)

Services on: Sundays at 18:30

77 Chorley New Road, Bolton BL6 4AQ

https://www.facebook.com/HorwichNSC

-

Hyde Spiritualist Church (SNU)

Services on: Mondays at 19:30

44 Great Norbury Street, Hyde, Cheshire SK14 1HY

https://www.facebook.com/HYDE-spiritualist-church-980546935443879

Leigh Spiritualist Temple (SNU)

Services on: Wednesdays at 19:30; Sundays at 15:00

3 Evans Street, Leigh, Lancashire WN7 1ES

https://www.facebook.com/LeighSpiritualistTemple

-

Liverpool Spiritualist Church (SNU)

Services on: Wednesdays at 19:30; Sundays at 18:30

14 Daulby Street, Liverpool L3 5NX

https://www.facebook.com/liverpoolspiritualistchurch/

-

Lotus of Peace at Kirkby

Services on: Tuesdays at 20:30

Kirkby ABC, (AKA Westvale youth and community centre) Richard Hesketh Drive, Kirkby L32 0TZ

https://www.facebook.com/Lotus-Of-Peace-at-Kirkby-107786598250992

-

Lotus of Peace Spiritualist Church

Services on: Sundays 19:30

Westhead Village Hall, Wigan Road, Ormskirk L40 6HZ

https://www.facebook.com/LotusOfPeaceSC

-

Luna Skys Crystals

Services on: Thursdays at 19:00

Clifton Community Centre, Wynne Avenue, Manchester M27 8FU

https://www.facebook.com/luna.skys.9216

Macclesfield Spiritualist Church (SNU)

Services on: Tuesdays at 19:30; Sundays at 18:30

18 Cumberland Street, Macclesfield, Cheshire SK10 1DD

https://www.facebook.com/macclesfieldspiritualistchurch

-

Manchester Spiritualist Church (SNU)

Services on: Tuesdays at 19:30; Sundays at 15:00

2 Alexandra Road South, Whalley Range, Manchester, Lancashire, M16 8ER

https://www.facebook.com/groups/274749949227340/

-

Middleton Spiritualist Church

Services on: Tuesdays at 19:30

Demesne Community Cente, Asby Close, Middleton, Oldham M24 4JF

https://www.facebook.com/groups/1472077669559653

-

Morecambe Temple of Light (SNU)

Services on: Saturdays at 19:00

West End Road, Morecambe LA4 4EF

https://www.facebook.com/groups/226495090734252

https://www.morecambe-temple-of-light-spiritualist-church.com

Moston Spiritualist Church (SNU)

Services on: Thursdays at 13:30; Mondays at 19:30

150 Church Lane, Moston, Manchester M9 4HZ

https://www.facebook.com/groups/mostonspiritualistchurch

-

Northwich Spiritualist Church (SNU)

Services on: Wednesdays at 19:30; Sundays at 18:30

Hadfield Street, Northwich CW9 5LU

https://www.facebook.com/groups/1050490631682550

http://northwichspiritualistchurch.co.uk

-

Oldham Spiritualist Church (SNU)

Services on: Mondays at 19:30

159 Ashton Rd, Oldham OL8 1LD

https://www.facebook.com/groups/oldhamspiritualist

-

Preston Ethical Spiritualist Church (SNU)

Services on: Tuesdays at 19:30; Sundays at 18:30

16 Newton Road, Preston PR2 1DY

https://www.facebook.com/PESC16/

Prestwich and Whitefield Spiritualist Church (SNU)

Services on: Wednesdays at 19:30; Sundays at 18:30

Prestwich Conservative Club, Church Lane, Prestwich M25 1AN

https://www.facebook.com/groups/145536528854796

-

Purple Light

Services on: Thursdays at 19:30

Unitarian Chapel, Park Street, Chorley PR7 1ER

https://www.facebook.com/lorraine.mackenzie.94617

-

Rawtenstall Spiritualist Centre (SNU)

Services on: Thursdays at 19:30

68-70 Newchurch Road, Rawtenstall, Lancashire BB4 7QX

https://www.facebook.com/rawtenstall.spiritualistchurch.7

-

Runcorn Spiritualist Church (SNU)

Services on: Wednesdays at 19:30; Sundays at 18:30

61 Ashridge Street, Runcorn WA7 1HU

https://www.facebook.com/runcorn.spiritualistchurch

-

Saddleworth Spiritualist Church (SNU)

Services on: Saturdays at 19:30

161 High St, Uppermill, Oldham OL3 6BY

https://www.facebook.com/groups/728152840601828

Salford Spiritualist Church (SNU)

Services on: Wednesdays at 19:30; Sundays at 18:30

129 Cross Lane, off Liverpool Street, Salford M5 4HH

https://www.facebook.com/SalfordSpiritualistChurch

-

Shaw Spiritualist Development Group (SNU)

Services on: Thursdays at 19:30

Voyager House, Duke St, Shaw, Oldham OL2 8PA

https://www.facebook.com/groups/267731633436371/

-

Skelmersdale Spiritualist Church

Services on: Wednesdays at 19:30

Ashurst Community Centre, Lyndhurst, Ashurst, Skelmersdale, Lancashire WN8 6QS

https://www.facebook.com/skelmersdaleindependentspiritualistcentre

-

Solway Spiritualist Group

Services on: Sundays at 18:30

Harrington Youth Club, Church Road, Harrington, Workington, Cumbria CA14 5PT

https://www.facebook.com/groups/245153978471/

SPIRIT ARK spiritual Group

Services on: Tuesdays at 19:30

Unitarian church corner of York Avenue, 57 Ullet Road, Liverpool L17 2AA

https://www.facebook.com/groups/273255312879738

-

St Annes Spiritual Society (SNU)

Services on: Thursdays at 19:30

Terrace Room, Inn on the Prom, Lytham St Annes FY8 1LU

https://www.facebook.com/groups/1743040819306193

-

St Francis Christian Spiritualist Church

Services on: not open at the moment

Edge Lane, Stretford, Manchester M32 8JD

http://zodiacs-children.com/

-

St Helens Spiritual Church (SNU)

Services on: Thursdays 14:00; Sundays at 18:30

20/22 Charles Street, Saint Helens WA10 1LH

https://www.facebook.com/St.Helens.Spiritualist.Church

-

St Stephens Christian Spiritualist Church

Services on: Wednesdays at 19:30

Community Room, Urmston (AFC) Football Club Meadowside, Davyhulme Road, Manchester M41 8QA

https://www.facebook.com/urmston.spiritualistchurch

Stockport Christian Spiritualist Church

Services on: Tuesdays at 19:30, Saturdays at 19:00, Sundays at 18:30

46 Old Road, Heaton Norris, Stockport SK4 1TD

https://www.facebook.com/Stockport-Christian-Spiritualist-Church-809257205801112

-

Stockport Spiritualist Church (SNU)

Services on: Tuesdays at 19:30

82 Chatham Street, Stockport SK3 9EG

https://www.facebook.com/stockportsnuspiritualistchurch/

-

The White Swans Spiritual Group

Services on: Sundays at 19:30

The Agnes Hopkins Centre, Claredon Road, Swinton, M27 4BQ

https://www.facebook.com/groups/490607204930993/

Trinity Spiritualist Group

Services on: Monthly on a Tuesday at 19:30

Dingle Community Learning Programme, 5 Shelmore Drive, Dingle, Liverpool L8 4YL

https://www.facebook.com/trinityspiritualistliverpool

Wallasey Spiritualist Church (SNU)

Services on: Tuesdays at 19:45; Sundays at 18:30

61 Withens Lane, Wallasey, Merseyside CH45 7NE

https://www.facebook.com/wallaseysnu

Warrington Spiritualist Church (SNU)

Services on: Sundays at 18:30

66 Academy Street, Warrington, Cheshire WA1 2BQ

https://www.facebook.com/SNUWarrington

-

Whispering Angels Astley

Services on: Sundays at 20:00

Astley, Tyldesley, Wigan M29 7DY

https://www.facebook.com/groups/1741951126105896/

-

Widnes Spiritualist Church (SNU)

Services on: Wednesdays at 19:00

1 Lacey St, Widnes, Cheshire WA8 7SQ

https://www.facebook.com/Spiritualist-church-Widnes-109393700520628

Woodhouse Park Spiritualist Church

Services on: Mondays at 20:00

Scout Hut, Braintree Road, Manchester M22 0HH

https://www.facebook.com/kevinsara123

Northern Ireland

Belfast Spiritualist Church (SNU)

Services on: Sundays at 18:30

134 Malone Avenue, Lisburn Road, Belfast BT9 6ET

https://www.facebook.com/Belfastspiritualist/

https://www.belfastspiritualistchurch.co.uk

-

Scotland

Aberdeen Spiritualist Centre & Healing Sanctuary (SNU)

Services on: Sundays at 11:15 and 18:15

71 Dee St, Aberdeen, AB11 6EE

https://www.facebook.com/deestreetaberdeen/

-

Ainglean Gheata Spiritualist Church

Services on: Sundays at 19:30

The Royal British Legion Club, Sanquhar Road, Forres IV361DG

https://www.facebook.com/groups/210664089348110/

-

Alloa Spiritualist Church

Services on: Sundays at 18:30

Alloa Old People Welfare Hall, 44 Erskine Street, Alloa, FK10 2AU

https://www.facebook.com/groups/AlloaSpiritualistChurch

Arbroath Spiritualist Centre (SNU)

Services on: Thursdays at 19:30

22 Commerce Street, Arbroath, Scotland DD11 1NB

https://www.facebook.com/groups/128487907179479

-

Armadale Church of Spiritual Light

Services on: Wednesdays at 19:30

Scout Hall, South Street, Armadale

https://www.facebook.com/groups/276052549257236

-

Arthur Conan Doyle Centre

Services on: Various through the week

25 Palmerston Place, Edinburgh, EH3 9AS

https://www.facebook.com/arthurconandoylecentre

https://www.arthurconandoylecentre.com/whats_on/

-

Ayr Spiritualist Centre (SNU)

Services on: Sundays at 18:30

10 Alloway Place, Ayr KA7 2AA

https://www.facebook.com/groups/1549344031943958/

Barrhead Spiritualist Church

Services on: Mondays at 19:00

ARC Aurs Drive, Barrhead G78 2LW

https://www.facebook.com/Barrhead-Spiritualist-Church-452805551843657

-

Bellshill and District Spiritualist Church

Services on: Tuesdays at 19:30

Bellshill Cultural Centre, Bellshill, Scotland ML4 1RJ

https://www.facebook.com/BellshillandDistrictSpiritualistChurch/

-

Bon-Accord Spiritualist Church (SNU)

Services on: Sundays at 11.15 and 18.15

37 Fraser Place, Aberdeen AB25 3TY

https://www.facebook.com/bonaccord.spirtualistchurch/

-

Cochrane Castle Spiritualist Centre

Services on: Tuesdays at 19:30

3 Burns Dr, Johnstone, Scotland PA5 0HJ

https://www.facebook.com/groups/1083412965025619/

-

Dumfries Spiritualist Church (SNU)

Services on: 2nd and 4th Saturday of a month at 19:00

Hallyday Hall, Lochvale House, Georgetown, Dumfries, Scotland DG1 4DF

https://www.facebook.com/groups/194465423912488

Dundee Church of the Spirit (SNU)

Services on: Wednesdays at 13:30; Sundays at 11:00

142 Nethergate, Dundee, Angus DD1 4EA

https://www.facebook.com/ChurchofthespiritDundee

-

Dundee Progressive Spiritualist Church (SNU)

Services on: not open at the moment

7 Artillery Lane, Dundee DD1 1PE

https://www.facebook.com/dundeeprogressivespiritualistchurch

-

Dunfermline Spiritualist Church (SNU)

Services on: Sundays at 18:00

3 Lady Campbells Walk, Dunfermline KY12 0QH

https://www.facebook.com/Dunfermlinespiritualistchurch

-

Edinburgh Association of Spiritualists (SNU)

Services on: Sundays at 11:00

25 Palmerston Place, Edinburgh EH125AP

https://www.facebook.com/edinburgh.spiritualists

Edinburgh College of Parapsychology (SNU)

Services on: Wednesdays at 14:30; Fridays at 19:30

2 Melville Street, Edinburgh EH3 7NS

https://www.facebook.com/Edinburgh-College-of-Parapsychology-434396273283445

http://www.edinburghpsychiccollege.com

-

Glasgow Association of Spiritualism (SNU)

Services on: occasional zoom services currently

6-7 Somerset Place, Sauchiehall Street, Glasgow G3 7JT

https://www.facebook.com/GASsomersetplace

-

Glasgow Central Spiritualist Church (SNU)

Services on: not open at the moment

64 Berkeley Street, Glasgow, Scotland G3 7DS

https://www.facebook.com/GlasgowCentralAssociationOfSpiritualistsBerkeleySt

-

Hamilton Spiritualist Church (SNU)

Services on: Thursdays at 19:30; Sundays at 18:30

19 Park Road, Hamilton, Lanarkshire, Scotland ML3 6PD

https://www.facebook.com/Hamilton-spiritualist-church-1838204823156927

Heavens Above Spiritualist Church

Services on: Tuesdays at 19:15

Dawson Centre, Bainsford, Falkirk FK2 7RG

https://www.facebook.com/groups/503383176976367

-

Inverness Spiritualist Church (SNU)

Services on: Mondays at 19:30

The Green Hall, Smithton, Inverness IV2 7NP

https://www.facebook.com/groups/Invernessspiritualchurch

-

Kilmarnock Spiritualist Church (SNU)

Services on: Mondays at 19:30; Sundays at 18:00

30 Old Mill Road, Kilmarnock KA1 3AW

https://www.facebook.com/kilmarnocksnu

https://www.kilmarnockspiritualistchurch.org

-

Kirkcaldy Spiritualist Centre (SNU)

Services on: Mondays at 19:00

Victoria House, 13 Kirk Wynd, Kirkcaldy, Fife, Scotland KY1 1EH

https://www.facebook.com/kirkcaldysc

Larkhall Spiritualist Church

Services on: Wednesdays at 19:30

Craigbank Primary School, Glengonnar Street, Larkhall, Scotland ML9 1EL

https://www.facebook.com/groups/900153016751063

-

Laurieston Spiritualist Church

Services on: Mondays at 19:30

Old Folks Welfare, Mary Street, Laurieston, Falkirk FK29PS

https://www.facebook.com/groups/419887388073836

-

Leading Lights Spiritualist Church

Services on: Fridays at 19:00

300 Napier Rd, Glenrothes KY6 1BF

https://www.facebook.com/The-leading-lights-spiritualist-church-114077123848796

-

Leven Valley Spiritual Church (Dumbarton Spiritualist Meetings)

Services on: Mondays at 19:30

Brock Bowling Green, Overturn Avenue, Dumbarton G82 2RD

https://www.facebook.com/groups/130702640404875

-

Light of Hope Spiritualist Church

Services on: Fridays at 19:30

Knightswood Community Centre, Alderman Road, Glasgow G13 3DD

https://www.facebook.com/groups/367208968420533

Livingston Spiritualist Church

Services on: Wednesdays at 19:30

Nether Dechmont Cottages, Carmondean Community Centre, Livingston EH54 8AX

https://www.facebook.com/livingston.spiritualist.church

-

Lochgelly Spiritualist Church (SNU)

Services on: Sundays at 17:00

37-39 Bank Street, Lochgelly, Fife, Scotland KY5 9QG

https://www.facebook.com/lochgellyspiritualist.church

-

Love And Light Spiritual & Wellbeing Centre

Services on: Sundays at 18:30

Unit 2B, Mains Road, Dundee DD3 7RH

https://www.facebook.com/LLSWCDUNDEE

https://www.loveandlightdundee.co.uk

-

New Falkirk Spiritualist Church

Services on: Alternate Saturdays ayt 19:00

Westfield Street, Falkirk FK2 9BW

https://www.facebook.com/NewFalkirkSpiritualistChurch

Pathhead and Dysart Spiritualist Church (SNU)

Services on: Sundays at 18:00

145 Commercial St, Kirkcaldy KY1 2NS

https://www.facebook.com/Pathhead-and-Dysart-Spiritualist-Church-2120835838144560

-

Perth Spiritualist Church (SNU)

Services on: Wednesdays at 19:00; Sundays at 18:30

Methven Buildings, 40 New Row, Perth, Perthshire, Scotland PH1 5QA

https://www.facebook.com/perth.sunchurch.9

-

Pleasance Spiritualist Church

Services on: Sundays at 19:00

Guide Hall, Pleasance, Falkirk FK1 1BG

https://www.facebook.com/groups/130447530356391

-

Shakespeare Spiritualist Church

Services on: Sundaya at 18:30

Shakespeare Street Youth Club, 95 Shakespeare Street, Maryhill, Glasgow G20 8LE

https://www.facebook.com/groups/shakespearechurch

Shetland First Spiritualist Church (SNU)

Services on: not open at the moment

Sound Hall, Lerwick, Shetland ZE1 0NP

https://www.facebook.com/ShetlandSpiritualists

-

Shininglight Spiritual Church

Services on: Fridays at 19:30

69 Langton Road, Pollok, Glasgow G53 5DD

https://www.facebook.com/carolineksusanl

-

Shotts Spiritualist Church

Services on: Tuesdays at 19:30

Community Centre Kirk Road, Shotts ML7 5ET

https://www.facebook.com/ShottsSpiritualistChurch

Sparkle of Light Spiritualist Church

Services on: 2 Sundays a month at 18:30

Rhu Shandon Community Centre, Hall Road, Rhu, Helensburgh G84 8RR

https://www.facebook.com/Sparkleoflightchurch

Spectral Knights Spiritual Centre

Services on: Sundays at 19:30

Grans Jean Hall, Long Lane, Grays, Thurrock RM16 2PJ

https://www.facebook.com/groups/652348805226742

Stars From Above Sanctuary

Services on: Wednesdays at 19:30

Prestwick Community Centre, Calaverock Road, Prestwick, Ayrshire KA9 1HP

https://www.facebook.com/groups/2146412028748946

-

Stevenston Spiritualist Centre

Services on: Mondays at 20:00

Hayhocks Community Centre, Hyslop Road, Stevenston KA20

https://www.facebook.com/groups/1860488050917075

-

Temple of Light Spiritualist Church

Services on: Wednesdays at 19:45

Nethermains Community Centre, Nethermains Road, Kilwinning KA13 6ES

https://www.facebook.com/groups/334625333366076/

-

The Angel Light Spiritualist Church

Services on: Fridays at 19:30

6 Daisy Street, Govanhill, Glasgow G42 8JL

https://www.facebook.com/groups/1386335844760782

-

The Little Robin Spiritualist Church

Services on: Thursdays at 19:30

The Institute, 37 Greenlees Road, Cambuslang G72 8JE

https://www.facebook.com/groups/963675960437719

The Tree Of Life Spiritual church

Services on: Wednesdays at 19:30

Spittal Community Hall, 2 Carrick Road, Rutherglen G73 4LJ

https://www.facebook.com/groups/689359091100209

-

The White Rose Spiritualist Sanctuary

Services on: Saturdays at 19:00

Oakbank Community Centre, Viewlands Road West, Perth PH1 1EJ

https://www.facebook.com/The-White-Rose-Spiritualist-Sanctuary-247222505476286

-

Unite Spiritualist Community Church Johnstone

Services on: Mondays at 19:15

Johnstone Castle Community Centre, Pine Cresent, Johnstone PA5 0BX

https://www.facebook.com/uscjohnstone/

-

White Dove Spiritualist Church

Services on: 1st and last Thursday of a month at 19:30

199 Prospecthill Circus, Glasgow G42 0LA

https://www.facebook.com/whitedovetoryglen

-

White Eagle Spiritualist Church

Services on: Tuesdays at 19:30

Broxburn Bowling Club, Longbyres off Station Road, Broxburn EH525TF

https://www.facebook.com/White-Eagle-Spiritualist-Church-188056434592810

Windygates Spiritualist Church

Services on: hoping to open by February 2022

Milton Road, Windygates, Leven KY8 5DG

https://www.facebook.com/groups/1449192468462021

Prayer for Release

I pray for release from all things past,
I pray for release from pain at last.
I pray for release from words remembered,
I pray for release from deeds surrendered.
I pray for release for the actions of others,
I pray for release from infidelity of lovers.
I pray for release from crimes good and bad,
I pray that release is a solution to be had.

Through Spiritual progression I know my fate,
Through Spiritual progression I know its never too late,
To learn from each and every restriction,
To know my own role in my own valediction.
Its only through my lessons learnt deep,
That a release is possible, a release to keep.

Veronica Jenkins

South East

Abingdon Spiritualist Church

Services on: Sundays at 18:15

Hadland Road Community Centre, Hadland Road, Abingdon, Oxfordshire OX14 3YH

https://www.facebook.com/abingdonspiritualistchurch

-

Amersham Spiritualist Church (SNU)

Services on: Fridays at 19:30

24 White Lion Road, Amersham HP7 9JD

https://www.facebook.com/AmershamSpirit/

-

Andover Spiritualist Fellowship (SNU)

Services on: Sundays at 18:30

Wellington Centre, Winchester Road, Andover SP10 2EG

https://www.facebook.com/groups/1758720194406989

-

Ashford Christian Spiritualist Church

Services on: Thursdays at 19:00; Saturdays at 18:30

Friends Meeting House, Albert Road, Ashford TN24 8NY

https://www.facebook.com/groups/ashfordchristianspiritualistchurch

Aylesbury Spiritualist Church (SNU)

Services on: Thursdays at 19:00

Mount Street, Aylesbury, Buckinghamshire HP20 2SE

https://www.facebook.com/aylesburyspiritualistchurch

https://aylesburyspiritual.wixsite.com/church

-

Barnham Spiritual Centre

Services on: Mondays at 19:30

Barnham Community Hall, Murrels Field, Yapton Road, Barnham PO22 0AY

https://www.facebook.com/Barnhamspiritualcentre

-

Basildon Spiritual Centre (ISM)

Services on: First Tuesday of every Month at 19:30

The George Hurd Activity Centre, Audley Way, Basildon, Essex SS14 2FL

https://www.facebook.com/groups/132886586783549

-

Basingstoke Spiritualist Church (SNU)

Services on: not reopened yet

28 Victoria Street, Basingstoke, Hampshire RG21 3BT

https://www.facebook.com/BasingstokeSC

Bexhill Christian Spiritualist Church

Services on: Sundays at 15:00

6 Victoria Road, Bexhill on Sea TN39 3PD

https://www.facebook.com/groups/830679733732056

Bexleyheath Christian Spiritualist Church

Services on: Tuesdays at 14:00; Sundays at 18:30

85 Lion Road, Bexleyheath, Kent DA6 8NT

https://www.facebook.com/Bexleyheath-Christian-Spiritualist-Church-681597208559613

-

Bicester Spiritualist Church

Services on: Sundays at 15:00

23 Ashdene Road, Bicester OX26 2BH

https://www.facebook.com/secretry.judithplowman

-

Billericay Spiritualist Centre (SNU)

Services on: Tuesdays at 20:00; First Sunday of a month at 18:30

16 West Park Crescent, Billericay, Essex CM12 9ED

https://www.facebook.com/BillericaySpiritualistCentre

https://billericayspiritualistcentre.org.uk

-

Bitterne Spiritualist Church (SNU)

Services on: Sundays at 18:30

390 Bitterne Rd, Bitterne, Southampton SO18 1DR

https://www.facebook.com/groups/2295153004058521

Bognor Regis Spiritual Centre (SNU)

Services on: Sundays at 18:30

7 Sudley Road, Bognor Regis PO21 1EJ

https://www.facebook.com/bognorspiritualistcentre7

-

Brighton & Hove National Spiritualist Church (SNU)

Services on: Sundays at 11:00

Edward Street, Brighton BN2 0JR

https://www.facebook.com/Brighton-Hove-National-Spiritualist-Church-192901794084920

http://brightonandhovenationalspiritualistchurch.com

-

Brotherhood Gate Spiritualist Centre (SNU)

Services on: Sundays at 17:00

21c St James Street, Brighton, BN2 1RF

https://www.facebook.com/Brotherhoodgate

-

Buckingham Spiritualist Church

Services on: 2nd Thursday of a month at 20:00; Sundays at 18:30

Buckingham Community Centre, Cornwalls Meadow, Buckingham MK18 1RP

https://www.facebook.com/Buckingham-Spiritualist-Church-495089497174044

Camberley Spiritualist Church (SNU)

Services on: Tuesdays at 19:30

112 Gordon Road, Camberley GU15 2JQ

https://www.facebook.com/CamberleySpiritualistChurch

Carterton Spiritualist Church

Services on: Tuesdays at 19:15

Brownes Hall, Brownes Lane, Carterton OX18 3JH

https://www.facebook.com/groups/579693012361845

Centre Of Love And Light

Services on: Sundays at 18:30

Old Blue Coats School, Chapel Street, Thatcham RG19 4QN

https://www.facebook.com/muriel.nunn

-

Chesham Spiritualist Centre

Services on: Fridays at 19:30

Sun House, 32 Church Street, Chesham HP5 1HU

https://www.facebook.com/CheshamSpiritualistCentre

-

Chesham Spiritualist Church

Services on: Thursdays at 19:30; Sundays at 18:30

Higham Road, Chesham, Bucks. HP5 2AF

https://www.facebook.com/Cheshamspiritualistchurch

https://www.spiritofchesham.org.uk

Cheshunt Spiritualist Church (SNU)

Services on: Wednesdays at 19:45; Sundays at 18:40

236-238 Turners Hill, Cheshunt, Waltham Cross EN8 9DD

https://www.facebook.com/groups/1441324995920756

-

Chichester Christian Spiritualist & Healing Centre

Services on: Thursdays at 19:30; Saturdays at 19:00; Sundays at 18:30

39 Basin Road, Chichester, West Sussex, PO19 8PY

https://www.facebook.com/groups/1540922642863417

-

Church of the Holy Spirit Whitstable

Services on: Occasional Saturdays at 19:00

81a Northwood Road, Tankerton, Whitstable CT5 2HD

https://www.facebook.com/churchoftheholyspiritwhitstable

http://www.churchoftheholyspiritwhitstable.com

-

Clacton-on-Sea Christian Spiritualist Church

Services on: Mondays at 14:15; Saturdays at 18:30

19 Oxford Road, Clacton-on-Sea, Essex CO15 3TB

https://www.facebook.com/groups/385322995741128

Corinthian Spiritualist Church and Healing Association

Services on: Sundays at 11:00

Primrose Hall, 15a London Road, Hailsham BN27 1EB

https://www.facebook.com/profile.php?id=100000928538691

http://www.corinthian-healing.co.uk

-

Cowes Spiritualist Church (SNU)

Services on: Sundays at 18:00

Newport Road, Cowes PO31 7PA

https://www.facebook.com/Cowes-Spiritualist-Church-393331387392633

-

Crawley Spiritualist Church (SNU)

Services on: Wednesdays at 19:30

Capel Lane, Gossops Green, Crawley, West Sussex RH11 8HL

https://www.facebook.com/crawley.spiritualistchurch

-

Dover Christian Spiritualist Church

Services on: Sundays at 18:30

Oddfellows, 29 Pencester Road,, Dover CT16 1BT

https://www.facebook.com/DoverSpiritualistChurch

East Grinstead Spiritual Community

Services on: 1st Sunday of a month at 11:00

The Old Court House, East Grinstead RH19 3LT

https://www.facebook.com/spiritualcommunity0

https://www.eastgrinsteadspiritualcommunity.com

Eastbourne Christian Spiritualist Church

Services on: Sundays at 15:00

1A Cavendish Ave, Eastbourne BN22 8EW

https://www.facebook.com/groups/705223160060101

-

Eastleigh Spiritualist Church (SNU)

Services on: Sundays at 18:30

Grantham Road, Eastleigh SO50 5PU

https://www.facebook.com/SpiritualistChurchEastleigh

-

Fleet Spiritualist Church (SNU)

Services on: Thursday at 19.30; Sundays at 18.30pm

193 Aldershot Road, Church Crookham, Fleet, Hampshire GU52 8JS

https://www.facebook.com/groups/123805881468196

-

Gillingham Spiritualist Church (SNU)

Services on: Wednesdays at 19:30; Sundays at 18:30

177 Canterbury Street, Gillingham, Kent ME7 5TU

https://www.facebook.com/groups/1469252933315196

-

Gosport Spiritualist Church (SNU)

Services on: Sundays at 18:30

183 Forton Road, Gosport, Hampshire PO12 4HB

https://www.facebook.com/Spiritualist-Church-of-Gosport-411934808997228

-

Gravesend Spiritualist Church (SNU)

Services on: Wednesdays at 19:30; Sundays at 18:30

19 Clarence Place, Gravesend DA12 1LD

https://www.facebook.com/Gravesend-Spiritualist-Church-612871232162397

-

Harlow and Epping Spiritual Sanctuary

Services on: Mondays at 14:00

Tye Green Community Centre, Bush Fair, Harlow CM18 6LU

https://www.facebook.com/groups/176843385701441

-

Harlow Spiritualist Centre

Services on: Sundays at 18:30

Maidmoore Room Great Parndon Community Centre, Abercrombie Way, Harlow CM18 6YJ

https://www.facebook.com/groups/300392973896606

Hastings Spiritualist Brotherhood Church (SNU)

Services on: Fridays at 19:30

Friends Meeting House, 5 South Terrace, Hastings TN34 1SA

https://www.facebook.com/groups/HastingsSNU

-

Havant Spiritualist Church (SNU)

Services on: Sundays at 18:30

10 The Tanneries, Brockhampton Lane, Havant PO9 1JB

https://www.facebook.com/Havant-Spiritualist-Church-106436922717460

http://havantspiritualistchurch.bravesites.com

-

Hayling Island Spiritualist Church

Services on: 1st Sunday of a month at 18:30

Gable Cladding, 17-19 Station Road, Hayling Island, PO11 0EA

https://www.facebook.com/hispiritualistchurch

-

Healing Angels Spiritual Centre

Services on: Tuesdays at 18:00

Village Hall, Church Road, Bulphan, Upminster RM14 3RU

https://www.facebook.com/Healing-Angels-103465518697121

https://www.healingangelsbulphan.co.uk

Hertford Spiritualist Church

Services on: 2nd Sunday of each month at 18:30; 4th Thursday of each month at 19:30

Quaker Rooms 50 Railway Street, Hertford SG14 1BA

https://www.facebook.com/hertfordspiritualistchurch

https://www.hertfordspiritualists.com/

-

Hitchin Spiritualist Church (SNU)

Services on: Once a month on a Wednesday at 19:30; alternate Sundays at 11:00

Whinbush Road, Hitchin, SG5 1PZ

https://www.facebook.com/groups/853995371301702

https://hitchinspiritualistchurch.co.uk

-

Hoddesdon Spiritualist Church (SNU)

Services on: Sundays at 18:30

Mayhem Function Hall, Brewery Road, Hoddesdon EN11 8HA

https://www.facebook.com/groups/1424870234450937

-

Horley Spiritualist Church

Services on: Tuesdays at 19:30

Strawson Community Hall, Albert Road, Horley RH6 7HZ

https://www.facebook.com/Horley-Spiritualist-Church-276460917510

Horsham Spiritual & Healing Centre

Services on: 4th Tuesday of a month at 19:30

The Normandy Centre, Denne Road, Horsham RH12 1JF

https://www.facebook.com/horshamspiritualandhealing

https://horshamspiritual.org

-

Houghton Regis Spiritualist Church

Services on: Thursdays at 19:30

Houghton Regis Memorial Hall, The Green, Houghton Regis, Dunstable LU5 5DX

https://www.facebook.com/Houghton-Regis-Spiritualist-Church-102443005402102

-

Hullbridge Spiritualist Church

Services on: Sundays at 18:00

238 Pooles Lane, Hullbridge, Hockley SS5 6ND

https://www.facebook.com/Hullbridge-Spiritualist-Church-2052413848102182

-

Hythe Christian Spiritualist Church

Services on: Sundays at 18:00

Mount Street, Hythe, Kent CT21 5NT

https://www.facebook.com/Hythe-Christian-Spiritualist-Church-1440216086213824

https://hythespiritualistchurch.co.uk

Hythe Spiritualist Church Independent

Services on: Fridays at 19:30

Hythe Community/Centre, Brinton Lane, Hythe Hants S045 6DU

https://www.facebook.com/groups/460144924318103

-

Karenza Spiritual Network

Services on: 1 Monday a month at 19:30

Cholsey Pavilion, Station Road, Cholsey, Wallingford OX10 9PT

https://www.facebook.com/KarenzaNetwork

http://www.karenzaspirit.net

-

Latchingdon Spiritualists

Services on: 1st and 3rd Fridays of a month at 20:00

Parish Hall, Burnham Road, Latchington, Chelmsford CM3 6EU

https://www.facebook.com/LatchingdonSpiritualists

Lechlade Independent Spiritualist Church

Services on: Thursdays at 19:30 (alternate weeks online and in church)

The Pavilion, Lechlade Memorial Hall, Lechlade, Oxfordshire GL7 3AY

https://www.facebook.com/groups/976350376231098

Littlehampton & Rustington Spiritualist Centre (SNU)

Services on: Sundays at 18:30

Scout Hall, Church Road, Rustington BN16 3NN

https://www.facebook.com/LASpiritualist

Maidenhead Spiritualist Church (SNU)

Services on: Thursdays at 19:30; Sunday at 18:30

River View Lodge, Ray Mead Road, Maidenhead SL6 8NJ

https://www.facebook.com/groups/241701379504670

-

Maidstone Independent Christian Spiritualist Church

Services on: Sundays at 18:30

100 Tonbridge Road, Maidstone, Kent, ME16 8JS

https://www.facebook.com/groups/MICSC

http://micsc.org.uk

-

Many Pathways Spiritualist Centre

Services on: Thursdays at 19:00

Minster Lovell Scout Hut, Brize Norton Road, Minster Lovell, Witney OX29 0SH

https://www.facebook.com/groups/249879628376698

-

North Oxford Christian Spiritualist Church

Services on: hoping to re-open May 2022

11a Middle Way, Summertown, Oxford OX2 7LH

https://www.facebook.com/northoxfordcsc

-

Oxford Christian Spiritualist Church (SNU & GW)

Services on: Sundays at 18:15

39A Oxford Road, Cowley, Oxford OX4 2EN

https://www.facebook.com/Oxford-Spiritualist-Church-642421835811345/

http://www.oxfordspiritualistchurch.com

-

Panshanger Spiritual Centre

Services on: Fridays at 20:00

Barndicott Hall, Barndicott, Panshanger, Welwyn Garden City AL7 2BS

https://www.facebook.com/hatfieldspiritualcentre

-

Portsmouth Temple of Spiritualism (SNU)

Services on: Sundays at 11:00

73A Victoria Road South, Southsea, Hampshire PO5 2BU

https://www.facebook.com/Portsmouth-Temple-of-Spiritualism-133760983306349

https://www.portsmouthtempleofspiritualism.co.uk

-

Rayleigh Spiritual & Healing Centre

Services on: Wednesdays at 19:00

WI Hall, Bellingham Lane, Rayleigh SS67ED

https://www.facebook.com/Rayleighspiritualcentre

-

Reading National Spiritualist Church (SNU)

Services on: Thursdays at 19:30; Sundays at 18:30

York Lodge 81 Baker Street, Reading RG1 7XY

https://www.facebook.com/groups/44011649777136

-

Sanctuary of Healing

Services on: Sundays at 18:30

Mills Terrace, Chatham ME4 5NZ

https://www.facebook.com/groups/115358072006

-

Shirley Spiritualist Church (SNU)

Services on: Sundays at 18:30

10 Grove Road, Shirley, Southampton SO15 3GG

https://www.facebook.com/groups/1037071916636004/

-

Slip End Spiritualist Church

Services on: Tuesdays at 19:30

Peter Edwards hall, off Church Road, Slip End nr Luton LU1 4BJ

https://www.facebook.com/groups/1623367904383460

-

Southampton Spiritualist Church (SNU)

Services on: Sundays at 11:00

Cavendish Grove, Southampton SO17 1XE

https://www.facebook.com/SouthamptonSpiritualistCentre

Spirit Links Stony Stratford

Services on: Monthly events

York House, Stony Stratford, Milton Keynes MK11 1JQ

https://www.facebook.com/groups/180869682085072

-

Spiritual Light Centre - Bletchley

Services on: Sundays at 18:30

Church Green Road, Bletchley, Milton Keynes MK3 6BJ

https://www.facebook.com/SpirituallightcentreBletchley

-

Spiritualist Church of Love and New Beginnings

Services on: Sundays at 18:30

Pettman House, The over 60's centre, Hanover Square, Herne Bay CT6 5NY

https://www.facebook.com/jill.goldfinchwaswillett

-

St Cecilia's Christian Spiritualist Church

Services on: Tuesdays at 19:30; Wednesdays at 14:30; Sundays at 18:30

9 Lord Roberts Avenue, Leigh-On-Sea SS9 1ND

https://www.facebook.com/StCecilias

-

Star of the East Hall

Services on: Fridays at 19:30; Sundays at 15:30

Edge End Road, Broadstairs CT10 2AH

https://www.facebook.com/Star-of-the-East-Hall-101664994694973

Strood Spiritual Centre

Services on: 2nd and 4th Sundays of a month at 18:30

Wainscott Memorial Hall, Holly Road, Wainscott, Kent ME2 4LG

https://www.facebook.com/stroodspiritualcentre

-

Swaythling Spiritualist Church (SNU)

Services on: Sundays at 18:30

Queen Elizabeth Court, 643 Portswood Road, Southampton SO17 3AJ

https://www.facebook.com/groups/462759220559560/

-

Tenterden Spiritualist Church

Services on: Alternate Saturdays at 18:30

Highbury Hall, Highbury Lane, Tenterden TN30 6LE

https://www.facebook.com/groups/1560543454191520/

-

The Betty Modestou Foundation, Pyramid of Light

Services on: 1st and 3rd Saturday of a month at 19:30

Willingdon Trees Community Centre, Holly Place, Eastbourne BN22 0UT

https://www.facebook.com/Thebettymodestoufoundationpyramidoflight

-

The Light Foundation

Services on: Saturdays at 19:30

233 Seaside Road, Eastbourne BN22 7NR

https://www.facebook.com/groups/770121076379106

Totton Spiritualist Church (SNU)

Services on: Sundays at 18:00

8 Rumbridge Street, Totton, Southampton SO40 9DP

https://www.facebook.com/totton.spiritualistchurch.1

Walking With Spirit Centre For Wannock Polegate

Services on: Monthly on a Friday at 19:30

Wannock Village Hall, Jevington Road, Polegate BN26 5NZ

https://www.facebook.com/groups/1824809541172348

-

Waterside Spiritual Centre

Services on: Monthly mediumhip evenings

14 Rockall Close, Lordshill, Southampton SO16 8BU

https://www.facebook.com/groups/471520113026323

-

Welwyn Garden Spiritualist Church (SNU)

Services on: Sundays at 18:30

Marsden Green, Welwyn Garden City, Hertfordshire AL8 6UZ

https://www.facebook.com/wgcspiritualistchurch

http://www.welwyngardencityspiritualistchurch.co.uk

-

Westcliff National Spiritualist Church (SNU)

Services on: Thursdays at 19:30; Sundays at 18:30

320 Westborough Road, Westcliff-on-Sea, Essex SS0 9PZ

https://www.facebook.com/groups/198089806922274

-

White Feather Spiritual Events

Services on: Thursdays at 19:30 (alternates with different venues)

Beckley Village Hall, Woodperry Road, Beckley, Oxford OX3 9UZ

Or

Bloxham Jubilee Park Hall, Barley Close, Bloxham OX15 4LW (occasional Sundays too)

Or

Witney Corn Exchange, Market Square, Witney, OX28 6AB

https://www.facebook.com/groups/245216352347640

-

White Rose Spiritualist Church

Services on: Sundays at 18:30

41 Sorrel Road, Oxford OX4 6SH

https://www.facebook.com/groups/196905413031

-

Winchester Independent Spiritualist Church

Services on: Sundays at 18:30

Somers Close, Winchester SO22 4

https://www.facebook.com/Winchester-Independent-Spiritualist-Church-103845631539770

http://www.spanglefish.com/WinchesterSpiritualistChurch

-

Windsor Spiritualist Church (SNU)

Services on: Sundays at 18:30

Adelaide Square, Windsor, West Berkshire SL4 2AQ

https://www.facebook.com/groups/624012807640082

http://www.windsorspiritualistchurch.co.uk

-

Witney Spiritualist Church

Services on: Sundays at 18:15

Burwell Hall, Thorney Leys, Witney OX28 5NP

https://www.facebook.com/groups/145219555492687

-

Woking Spiritualist Church (SNU)

Services on: Thursdays at 19:30; Sundays at 18:30

Grove Road, Woking, GU21 5JB

https://www.facebook.com/Woking-Spiritualist-Church-111276561321547

http://www.wokingspiritualistchurch.co.uk

-

Wokingham Spiritualist Church

Services on: Wednesdays at 19:30

Quakers Meeting Rooms, 28 Denton Road, Wokingham RG40 2DX

https://www.facebook.com/wokinghamsc

-

Woolston Spiritual Centre

Services on: Fridays at 19:00

The Scout Hut, 261 Spring Road, Sholing, Southampton SO19 2NZ

https://www.facebook.com/groups/WSCwithHSM

-

Worthing Spiritualist Church

Services on: Sundays at 11:00

Grafton Road, Worthing BN11 1QY

https://www.facebook.com/Worthing-Spiritualist-Church-Grafton-Road-298566243541993

http://worthing-spiritualist.org.uk

South West

Bedminster Spiritualist Church (SNU)

Services on: Tuesdays at 14:15; Sundays at 18:30

74A Chessel Street, Bristol, BS3 3DN

https://www.facebook.com/Bedminsterspiritualistchurch

-

Ben's Place for Spirituality

Services on: Events monthly online and in centre

Ben's Place Spiritual Centre, Oxford Road, Garsington, Oxford OX44 9AU

https://www.facebook.com/Bens-Place-centre-for-Spirituality-108398621056388

-

Bideford Centre of Light (SNU)

Services on: Saturdays at 18:30; Sundays at 18:30

Hart Street, Bideford EX39 2LB

https://www.facebook.com/Bideford-Centre-of-light-751817121534695

-

Bluebell Spiritualist Church Chippenham

Services on: Wednesdays at 19:30

Sheldon School, Hardenhuish Lane, Chippenham SN14 6HJ

https://www.facebook.com/bluebellspiritualistchurch.chippenham

-

Bodmin Spiritualist Church & Healing Centre (SNU)

Services on: Tuesdays at 19:30

57 Higher Bore Street, Bodmin PL31 1JS

https://www.facebook.com/Bodminsc

http://www.bodminspirit.uk

-

Bournemouth Spiritualist Church (SNU)

Services on: Thursdays at 15:00; Sundays at 10:45

16 Bath Road, Bournemouth BH1 2PE

https://www.facebook.com/bournemouth123

http://www.bsnuc.co.uk/index.html

-

Brixham United Spiritualist Church

Services on: Sundays at 18:00

Chestnut Community Centre, 1-3 Poplar Close, Brixham, Devon TQ5 0SA

https://www.facebook.com/groups/119828488059816

-

Brunswick Spiritualist Church (SNU)

Services on: Thursdays at 19:00; Sundays at 15:00

1 Keppel Place, Stoke, Plymouth, Devon PL2 1AX

https://www.facebook.com/BrunswickPlymouth

-

Budleigh Salterton Spiritual Centre

Services on: 2nd Friday of each month at 19:30

Venture Hall, Budleigh Salterton EX9 6QE

https://www.facebook.com/Budleigh-Salterton-Spiritual-Centre-1215833195113566

-

Butterfly Lodge Spiritualist Church

Services on: Sundays at 18:30

Page Community Hall, Page Road, Staple Hill, Bristol BS16 4NE

https://www.facebook.com/groups/302915730295404

-

Camborne Christian Spiritualist Church

Services on: Sundays at 18:30

The Ex-registry Office, Roskear, Camborne TR14 8DN

https://www.facebook.com/cambornechristianspiritualistchurch.org

-

Charminster Spiritualist Church

Services on: Saturdays at 19:00; First Tuesday of a month at 15:00

207 Charminster Road, Bournemouth BH8 9QQ

https://www.facebook.com/Charminster-Spiritualist-Church-Events-195871597593314

-

Cheltenham Spiritualist Church (SNU)

Services on: Sundays at 11:00

19 Bennington Street, Cheltenham GL50 4ED

https://www.facebook.com/CheltenhamSpiritualistChurch

-

Chippenham First Spiritualist Church (SNU)

Services on: Wednesdays at 19:00

Kingsley Road Community Hall, Kingsley Road, Chippenham, Wiltshire SN140AS

https://www.facebook.com/chippenham.firstspiritualistchurch

-

Christchurch Spiritualist Centre (SNU)

Services on: Thursdays at 19:30; Sundays at 10:45

196B Barrack Rd, Christchurch BH23 2BQ

https://www.christchurchsc.org.uk

-

Dawlish Psychic and Spiritual Centre Guiding Light

Services on: Alternate Tuesdays at 19:30

The Manor House & Riverside Centre, Old Town Street, Dawlish EX7 9AP

https://www.facebook.com/groups/Guidinglightdawlish

-

Enchanted Holistic Events

Services on: Monthly on Saturdays at 19:00

High Ham Village Hall, High Ham TA10 9DA

https://www.facebook.com/somersetfayres/

Eternal Spirit

Services on: Thursdays at 19:30

Foxhole Community Centre, Belfield Road, Paignton TQ3 3UZ

https://www.facebook.com/profile.php?id=100057549703776

-

Exeter Spiritualist Centre & Healing group (SNU)

Services on: Wednesdays at 13:30; Sundays at 18:30

York Road, Exeter, Devon EX4 6PF

https://www.facebook.com/elthamspiritualchurch

https://www.exeterspiritualistcentre.org

-

Falmouth Central Christian Spiritualist Church

Services on: Tuesdays at 14:30; Saturdays at 19:30; Sundays at 18:30

2 Quarry Hill, Falmouth TR11 2BP

https://www.facebook.com/falchurch

-

Footsteps Clairvoyance

Services on: Mondays at 19:30

G.D.A Community Centre, Colin Road, Barnwood, Gloucester GL4 3JL

https://www.facebook.com/FOOTSTEPSGLOS1/

-

Gloucester National Spiritualist Church (SNU)

Services on: Sundays at 11:00

2a Brunswick Square, Gloucester GL1 1UG

https://www.facebook.com/groups/935819769872507

-

Heaven Sent Spiritual Centre

Services on: Once a month on a Monday at 19:00

Wapley Riding Stables, Wapley Hill, Westerleigh, Bristol BS37 8RJ

https://www.facebook.com/groups/Heavensentspiritualcentre

https://www.heavensentspiritualcentre.co.uk

-

Hillsborough Spiritualist Church (SNU)

Services on: Saturdays at 19:00; Sundays at 11:00

Pearson Road, Mutley, Plymouth, Devon PL4 7DH

https://www.facebook.com/HillsboroughSpiritualistChurchPlymouth

-

Knowle Spiritualist Church

Services on: Sundays at 18:30

Redcatch Community Centre, Redcatch Road, Knowle, Bristol BS4 2EP

https://www.facebook.com/groups/524000067759483

-

Melksham Spiritualist Centre

Services on: Sundays at 18:00

The Scouts Hall, King George V Playing Fields, Melksham SN12 6LP

https://www.facebook.com/Melksham-Spiritualist-Centre-191274377589954

http://www.melkshamspiritualcentre.com

-

Moonbeams

Services on: Wednesdays at 19:30

The Avenue Hotel, Bristol Road, Gloucester GL1 5TH

https://www.facebook.com/groups/309698952468574

-

Newton Abbot Spiritualist Church (SNU)

Services on: Wednesdays at 19:30; Sundays at 18:30

East Street, Newton Abbot TQ12 1AQ

https://www.facebook.com/groups/121220707921281

-

One Heart United Spiritualist Church

Services on: Fridays at 19:30; Sundays at 18:30

The Acorn Centre, Lummaton Cross, Torquay TQ2 8ET

https://www.facebook.com/groups/473295580794139

-

Oreston Crusader Fellowship

Services on: Sundays at 18:30

5 Oreston Road, Oreston, Plymouth PL9 7JZ

https://www.facebook.com/CrusaderFellowshipChristianSpiritualistChurch

-

Paignton SNU Spiritualist Centre (SNU)

Services on: Mondays at 19:30; Wednesdays at 14:00; Sundays at 11:00

30 Manor Road, Paignton TQ3 2JB

https://www.facebook.com/groups/339297059461856

-

Penzance Spiritualist Church

Services on: 1st Thursday of a month at 19:00

20 Bread Street, Penzance, Cornwall TR18 2EH

https://www.facebook.com/Penzance-Spiritualist-Church-1712489965631477

Poole Christian Spiritualist Church

Services on: Sundays at 11:00

18 Kingland Road, Poole, BH15 1TP

https://www.facebook.com/poolespiritualists

Portishead Spiritualist Church

Services on: Wednesdays at 19:30

Brampton Pre-School Hall, Brampton Way, Portishead, Bristol BS20 6YN

https://www.facebook.com/Portishead-Spiritualist-Church-598537610158956

Ringwood Christian Spiritualist Church

Services on: Sundays at 18:00

St. Leonards & St.Ives Village Hall, Braeside Road, St. Leonards BH24 2PH

https://www.facebook.com/Ringwood-Christian-Spiritualist-Church-112034857373702/

Ryde Spiritualist Church (SNU)

Services on: zoom only currently

28 Belvedere Street, Ryde, Isle of Wight PO33 2JW

https://www.facebook.com/RydeSpiritualistChurch

Salisbury Spiritualist Meeting House (SNU)

Services on: Sundays at 18:30

106 Wilton Road, Salisbury SP2 7JJ

https://www.facebook.com/SalisburySpiritualistMeetingHouse

Soundwell Road Spiritualist Church (SNU)

Services on: Monthly Saturdays at 19:30; Sundays at 18:30

123 Soundwell Road, Soundwell, Bristol BS16 4RD

https://www.facebook.com/soundwellroadchurch

-

Stroud Spiritualist Church

Services on: Fridays at 19:30; Sundays at 18:30

Lansdown, Stroud GL5 1BB

http://www.stroudspiritualistchurch.org

Swindon Spiritualist Centre and Healing Sanctuary (SNU)

Services on: Sundays at 18:30

31 Devizes Road, Swindon SN1 4BG

https://www.facebook.com/SwindonSpiritualistCentreAndHealingSanctuary

-

Taunton New Spiritualist Church

Services on: Sundays at 18:30

Staplegrove Village Hall, 214 Staplegrove Road, Taunton TA2 6AL

https://www.facebook.com/spiritualstchurch

-

The Church of the Holy Spirit

Services on: Sundays at 18:30

Kings Avenue, St Austell PL25 4TT

https://www.facebook.com/groups/731377767045777

https://thelittlechurch.co.uk

-

The Cornwall Corinthian Centre

Services on: 2nd and 4th Sundays of a month at 18:30

The Richard Jory Hall, Frogpool, Cornwall TR4 8SA

https://www.facebook.com/groups/308678553305622

-

The Light Spiritualist Church

Services on: Tuesdays at 19:00, Sundays at 18:15

Preston Village Hall, Preston Road, Weymouth DT3 6BH

https://www.facebook.com/wendy.wharton.39

-

The New Christian Spiritualist Church Swanage

Services on: 3rd Tuesday of a month at 14:00

Queensmead, Queens Road, Swanage BH19 2PS

https://www.facebook.com/szalkai26/

-

Tiverton Christian Spiritualist Church

Services on: Sundays at 18:30

Gold Street, Tiverton EX16 6QB

https://www.facebook.com/Tiverton-Christian-Spiritualist-Church-111678611316880

-

Tiverton Spiritual and Healing Group

Services on: Alternate Tuesdays at 19:30

The Memorial Hall, Angel Hill, Tiverton EX16 6PA

https://www.facebook.com/tivertonspiritual

-

Ventnor Spiritualist Church (SNU)

Services on: Sundays at 18:00

8 Victoria Street, Ventnor, Isle of Wight PO38 1ET

https://www.facebook.com/Ventnor-spiritualist-church-174072852649778

Westbury Park Spiritualist Church (SNU)

Services on: Sundays at 11:00 and 18:30

Cairns Road (Kellaway Road End), Bristol BS6 7TH

https://www.facebook.com/WestburyParkSpiritualistChurch

https://westburyparkspiritualistchurch.org/services

-

Weston-Super-Mare National Spiritualist Church (SNU)

Services on: Sundays at 15:00

2 Stafford Road, Weston-super-Mare BS23 3BW

https://www.facebook.com/wsmspiritualistchurch

-

Weymouth Community Spiritual Centre

Services on: Sundays at 18:00

The Moose Lodge, Chickerell Road, Weymouth DT4 0BW

https://www.facebook.com/Weymouth-Community-Spiritual-Centre-110287024594132

-

Wilton Spiritualist Church (SNU)

Services on: Sundays at 18:30

3 Warminster Road, Wilton, Salisbury SP2 0AT

https://www.facebook.com/groups/wiltonspiritualistchurch

Wales

2 Feathers Penrhiwceiber /Penderyn

Services on: Sundays once a month at 18:30

The Community Hall, Penderyn CF44 9UX

https://www.facebook.com/groups/257511031098213

-

Aberaeron Spiritualist Church

Services on: Saturdays at 14:30

Aberaeron Spiritualist Church, Waterloo Street, Aberaeron, Ceredigion SA46 0BW

https://www.facebook.com/AberaeronSpiritualistChurch

-

Aberkenfig Spiritualist Church (SNU)

Services on: Thursdays at 19:00; Sundays at 18:00

Pandy Park, Aberkenfig, Bridgend, Mid Glamorgan CF32 9RE

https://www.facebook.com/AberkenfigSNU

-

Abersychan Spiritualist Centre

Services on: Sundays at 19:00

Victoria Village Community Hall, Cwmavon Road, Abersychan, Pontypool NP4 8PU

https://www.facebook.com/groups/124877491180579

Barry National Spiritualist Church & Centre (SNU)

Services on: Sundays at 18:00

Buttrills Road, Barry, South Glamorgan CF62 8EF

https://www.facebook.com/BarrySNU

-

Blackwood Spiritualist Church (SNU)

Services on: Wednesdays at 19:00; Sundays at 18:00

204 High Street, Blackwood, Wales NP12 1AJ

https://www.facebook.com/Blackwood-Spiritualist-Church-106197305103146

-

Bridgend Spiritualist Church (SNU)

Services on: Sundays at 18:00

Bridgend National Spiritualists Church, The Rhiw, Bridgend CF31 3BL

https://www.facebook.com/bridgendspiritualistchurch

-

Cadoxton Christian Spiritualist Church

Services on: Sundays at 18:30

29 Kenilworth Road, Barry CF63 2HB

https://www.facebook.com/groups/149307874296

-

Caerleon Spiritualist Centre

Services on: Thursdays at 19:30

Town Hall, Church Street, Caerleon, NP18 1AW

https://www.facebook.com/groups/CaerleonSpiritualistCentre

Cardiff Spiritualist Church and Healing Centre (SNU)

Services on: zoom only currently

20 Park Grove, Cardiff, Wales CF10 3BN

https://www.facebook.com/Cardiff-SNU-Spiritualist-Church-and-Healing-Centre-111090667217731

-

Circle of Spiritual Friendship - Black Park

Services on: Mondays at 19:30

Black Park Community Centre, Chirk LL14 5BB

https://www.facebook.com/profile.php?id=1774186881

-

Circle of Spiritual Friendships - Wrexham

Services on: Wednesdays at 19:30

Maesgwyn Community Centre, Lilac Way, Wrexham LL11 2AJ

https://www.facebook.com/groups/247783969171781

-

Colwyn Bay Spiritualist Church (SNU)

Services on: Saturdays at 19:00

17 Woodland Road West, Colwyn Bay LL29 7DH

http://colwynbayspiritualistchurch.sites.k-hosting.co.uk/

-

Cwm Spiritualist Church (SNU)

Services on: not open at the moment

River Row, Cwm, Ebbw Vale NP23 7TJ

https://www.facebook.com/RiverRowNP237TJ

Cwmbran Spiritual Centre

Services on: Tuesdays at 19:30

The Threepenny Bit, Deerbrook, Fairhill, Cwmbran NP44 4SX

https://www.facebook.com/groups/185957678225384

-

Gateway Christian Spiritualist Church

Services on: Sundays at 18:30

2a Northcote Street, Roath, Cardiff CF24 3BH

https://www.facebook.com/Gatewaychurchcardiff

https://www.gatewaycschurch.co.uk

-

Gorseinon Spiritualist Church

Services on: 1st Saturday of each month at 19:00

Gorseinon Institute, Lime Street, Gorseinon, Swansea SA4 4AD

https://www.facebook.com/groups/1419223861636872

-

Griffithstown Spiritual Church

Services on: Mondays at 19:45

Skippys Bar, 3 Charles St, Griffithstown, Pontypool NP4 5HG

https://www.facebook.com/groups/4618309991564751

Holyhead Spiritualist Association

Services on: Thursdays at 19:00

Millbank Community Centre, Bryn Gwyn Road, Holyhead LL65 1TE

https://www.facebook.com/Holyhead-Spiritualist-Association-463258417543405/

Little Mill Spiritualist Church

Services on: 1st Thursday of a month at 19:30

Little Mill Village Hall, Berthon Road, Little Mill, Pontypool NP4 0HJ

https://www.facebook.com/groups/621657798580342

-

Llanbradach Christian spiritualist church

Services on: Wednesday at 19:00

OAP Welfare Hall, 36 High St, Llanbradach, Caerphilly CF83 3LQ

https://www.facebook.com/groups/660706487973205

-

Merthyr Tydfil Temple Spiritualist Church (SNU)

Services on: Tuesdays at 19:30

Pontmorlais W, Merthyr Tydfil CF47 8UN

https://www.facebook.com/SpiritualistChurchMTTemple

-

New Dawn Holistic spiritual and healing centre

Services on: alternate Wednesdays at 19:30

Caerau Development Trust (Community Centre) Woodland Terrace, Caerau, CF34 0SR

https://www.facebook.com/groups/463403420684651

Oxford Street Spiritualist Church

Services on: Wednesdays at 19:00; Sundays at 18:15

Oxford Street, Swansea SA1 3AN

https://www.facebook.com/groups/17653333015

-

Panteg Spiritualist group

Services on: Wednesdays at 19:00

Panteg Employee Club, Grithstown, Pontypool NP4 5BE

https://www.facebook.com/groups/452114829097113

-

Pontywaun Spiritualist Church

Services on: not open at the moment

Halls Road Terrace, Pontywaun, Caerphilly NP117FQ

https://www.facebook.com/groups/321976444914263

-

Port Talbot Spiritualist Church (SNU)

Services on: Thursdays at 19:00; Sundays at 18:00

1 Ty-draw Place, Port Talbot, West Glamorgan SA13 1JZ

https://www.facebook.com/Port-Talbot-Spiritualist-Church-1938699653120703

Psychic Ability

Services on: Tuesdays at 19:30

New Panteg RFC, New Road Pontypool NP40TL

-

Rainbowmoon Spiritual Centre

Services on: Wednesdays at 18:30; Sundays at 18:30

Good Companions Club, Archibald Street, Newport NP19 8ER

https://www.facebook.com/donna.nail.98

-

Rhyl Spiritualist Centre (SNU)

Services on: Thursdays at 19:00

Ffordd Las community centre, 20 Ffordd Las, Rhyl LL18 2EB

https://www.facebook.com/groups/188599664532283

-

Ruabon Spiritualist Church

Services on: Tuesdays at 19:15

The Ruabon Spiritualist Centre The Village Hall Ruabon LL146AA

https://www.facebook.com/ruabonspiritualistcentre

-

Rumney Spiritualist Church

Services on: Sundays at 19:30

Rumney Memorial Hall, Wentloog Road, Rumney, Cardiff CF3 3EA

https://www.facebook.com/groups/1054176678094435

Simply Spiritual Cwmbran

Services on: Fridays at 19:00

Thornhill Community Centre, Leadon Court, Cwmbran NP445TZ

https://www.facebook.com/SimplySpiritualCwmbran/

-

Simply Spiritualist Church

Services on: Mondays at 19:00

O.A.P.Hall, Tyntyla Road, Ystrad, Rhondda CF41 7SF

https://www.facebook.com/profile.php?id=100057237926890

http://simplyspiritualistchurch.co.uk

-

St Johns Christian Spiritualist Church

Services on: Sundays at 18:30

1 Haulwen Road, Cockett, Swansea SA2 0GG

https://www.facebook.com/St-Johns-Christian-Spiritualist-Church-400632146810532

-

Tenby Healing Time Spiritualist Church

Services on: First Sunday of month at 19:15

New Hedges Village Hall, New Hedges, Tenby, Pembrokeshire SA70 8TN

https://www.facebook.com/groups/439767492726971

-

The Breath of Life Foundation

Services on: Fridays at 19:30

Carmarthen Scout Hall, Woods Row, Carmarthen SA31 1BU

https://www.facebook.com/groups/1216143982194050

-

The Wyesham Group of the Monmouth Society of Spiritual Awareness & Church

Services on: First and last Sunday of a month at 18:30

St. James' Hall, Wyesham, Monmouth NP25 3JY

https://www.facebook.com/The-Wyesham-Group-of-the-Monmouth-Society-of-Spiritual-Awareness-Church-393227087423259

-

Tredegar Trinity Spiritualist Church

Services on: Wednesdays at 19:00; Sundays at 18:00

Gelli Road, Tredegar, Wales NP22 3RD

https://www.facebook.com/Tredegar-Trinity-Spiritualist-Church-434662053367234

-

Treforest Spiritualist Church (SNU)

Services on: Monthly Sundays at 18:00

Cyrch Y Gwas Road, Treforest, Pontypridd, Mid Glamorgan CF37 1SH

https://www.facebook.com/treforestspiritualist

Willow Spiritualist Group

Services on: Tuesdays at 20:00

Kingsland Center, Clifton Terrace, Holyhead LL65 2SL

https://www.facebook.com/groups/308187695488

Wrexham Spiritualist Group

Services on: Sundays at 19:15

St Peters Hall, Smithfield Road, Wrexham LL13 8ER

https://www.facebook.com/wrexhamspiritualgroup

-

Wyesham Group

Services on: Sundays at 18:30

St. James' Hall, Wyesham, Monmouth. NP25 3JY

https://www.facebook.com/groups/241278262594370

Prayer of Passing
My prayer for you this day is a smooth and peaceful passing,
I pray for your release from pain and a celebratory home coming to the world of eternity.

My prayer for you this day is a gentle drifting off to sleep,
A release from the old you to your timeless eternal being.

My prayer for you this day is that the love we shared this lifetime,
Takes you safely into the arms of loved ones and angels who are waiting.

My prayer for you this day is that the highs and lows of this life have helped your Spiritual journey
That the lessons you have learnt here will travel with you.

My prayer to you this day is that you will come to visit me from time to time
To make your presence known to me when I need your comfort most.

My prayer for me this day is that I will hear your voice on the wind, see your presence in a feather
And feel your love around me until we meet once again in eternity.

Blessings Be   Veronica Jenkins

West Midlands

Angel Serenity

Services on: Wednesdays at 19:15

The Jubilee Crescent Community Centre, Radford, Coventry

https://www.facebook.com/lee.greenwood.73113

-

Bilston Christian Spiritualist Church (GW)

Services on: Wednesdays at 19:30

15 Broad Street, Bilston WV14 0BP

https://www.facebook.com/Bilston-Christian-Spiritualist-Church-1805686866422816

-

Bloxwich Temple of Light (SNU)

Services on: Wednesdays at 19:30; Sundays at 18:30

Revival Street, Bloxwich, Walsall WS3 3HL

https://www.facebook.com/bloxwich.snu.18

Blue Lodge Droitwich

Services on: Tuesdays at 19:45

The Barn, New Chawson Lane, Droitwich WR9 0AQ

https://www.facebook.com/groups/146041270922

Blue Lodge Worcester

Services on: Mondays at 19:45

KGV Community Hub, Ash Avenue, Brickfields Rd, Worcester WR4 9TL

https://www.facebook.com/bluelodgespiritualist.churchworcester/

Bromsgrove Spiritualist Church (SNU)

Services on: Sundays at 18:30 (2nd and 4th of month); alternate Wednesdays at 19:30

20 Church Road, Catshill, Bromsgrove, Worcestershire B61 0JY

https://www.facebook.com/groups/100641939975791

-

Brownhills Excelsior Spiritualist Church (SNU)

Services on: Thursdays at 19:30; Sundays at 18:30

High Street, Brownhills, Walsall, West Midlands WS8 6HL

https://www.facebook.com/brownhillsexcelsiorSC

-

Burslem Spiritualist Church (SNU)

Services on: Sundays at 15:00

87 Hayward Road, Burslem, Stoke on Trent, Staffordshire ST6 7AH

https://www.facebook.com/groups/1530164123938676

-

Coventry Broadgate National Spiritualist Church (SNU)

Services on: Thursdays at 13:30 and 19:30

Eagle Street, Coventry CV1 4GP

https://www.facebook.com/broadgatespiritualistchurch

Darlaston Spiritualist Church (SNU)

Services on: Sundays at 18:30

11 Pinfold Street Extension, Darlaston, Wednesbury WS10 8PU

https://www.facebook.com/H34ler2017

https://www.darlastonspiritualistchurchofficialwebsite.org

-

Dudley Spiritualist Centre (SNU)

Services on: Thursdays at 19:30

33 Paradise, Dudley DY2 8SH

https://www.facebook.com/Dudley-Spiritualist-Centre-Paradise-Buffery-Park-113794049998593

-

Evesham Spiritualist Church

Services on: 2nd and 4th Sunday of the month at 18:00

Unitarian Chapel, Oat Street, Evesham, Worcs WR11 4RY

https://www.facebook.com/groups/147853295241786

-

Fenton Spiritualist Church (SNU)

Services on: Sundays at 18:30

60/62 King Street, Fenton, Stoke On Trent, ST4 3ET

https://www.facebook.com/fentonchurchstoke

-

Foleshill Spiritualist Church

Services on: Last Thursday of a month at 19:30; Sundays at 15:00

Broad Street, Foleshill, Coventry CV6 5AZ

https://www.facebook.com/groups/410620652327700

-

Forget me Not Spiritual Centre

Services on: Sundays at 10:30

Westfields Community Hall, Highmore Street, Hereford

https://www.facebook.com/groups/313509213817817

-

Golden Light Spiritualist Church

Services on: Sundays at 18:30

Bevon Lee Community Centre, 28 Bevan Lee Road, Cannock WS11 4PS

https://www.facebook.com/groups/602580526586899

-

Hall Green Independent Spiritualist Church

Services on: Wednesdays at 13:30; Sundays at 18:30

York Road, Hall Green, Birmingham B28 8LH

https://www.facebook.com/profile.php?id=100073440801390

-

Harborne Healing Centre

Services on: Saturdays at 19:00; Sundays at 18:30

144-146 Weoley Park Road, Selly Oak, Birmingham B29 5HA

https://www.facebook.com/Harborne-Healing-Centre-1770832683148306

Hinckley National Spiritualist Church (SNU)

Services on: Wednesdays at 14:00; Tuesdays at 19:30; Sundays at 18:00

32 Station Road, Hinckley LE10 1AW

https://www.facebook.com/groups/581316268619653

-

Kings Heath National Spiritualist Church (SNU)

Services on: Saturdays at 19:30; Sundays at 18:30

5 Springfield Road, Kings Heath, Birmingham, B14 7DT

https://www.facebook.com/KingsHeathNationalSpiritualistChurch

-

Leamington National Spiritualist Church (SNU)

Services on: Wednesdays at 14:30; Sundays at 18:00

1 Holly Street, Leamington Spa, Warwickshire CV32 4TN

https://www.facebook.com/Leamington-Spa-SNU-Church-1598547377123444

-

Longton National Spiritualist Church (SNU)

Services on: Sundays at 18:30

1 Normacot Road, Stoke-On-Trent, Staffordshire ST3 1PR

https://www.facebook.com/longtonnationalspiritualistchurch95

https://www.longtonspiritualistchurch.com

-

Newcastle Christian Spiritualist Church

Services on: Saturdays at 18:30; Sundays at 18:30

Corner Of Hanover Street & Hassell Street, Newcastle-under-Lyme ST5 1AU

https://www.facebook.com/groups/441382463052232

-

Nuneaton Spiritualist Church (SNU)

Services on: Mondays at 19:30; Sundays at 18:00

Norman Avenue, Nuneaton, Warwickshire CV11 5NZ

https://www.facebook.com/Nuneaton-Spiritualist-Church-911443882330213

-

Parkside Spiritualist Church (SNU)

Services on: Sundays at 15:00

4 MacDonald Road, Wyken, Coventry CV2 5FF

https://www.facebook.com/parksidespiritualist.church.3

-

Redditch Spiritualist Centre (SNU)

Services on: Wednesdays at 19:30; Sundays at 11:00

139 Easemore Road, Redditch B98 8HU

https://www.facebook.com/RedditchSpiritualistCentre

https://www.redditchspiritualistcentre.co.uk/weekly-activities-2

Rugby Independent Spiritualist Church

Services on: Sundays at 18:30

Pennington Mews, Rugby CV21 2RG

https://www.facebook.com/Rugby.Spiritualist.Church

Smethwick Spiritualist Church (SNU)

Services on: Thursdays at 19:30

152 Thimblemill Road, Smethwick, Birmingham B67 5RG

https://www.facebook.com/SmethwickSpiritualist/

https://www.smethwickspiritualistchurch.com

Soul to Soul Spiritual Connections

Services on: Mondays at 19:30

Drayton Lane, Drayton Bassett, Tamworth B78 3TS

https://www.facebook.com/Soul-to-soul-spiritual-connections-548505019013323

Southam Spiritualists

Services on: Last Sunday of a month at 19:30

The Grange, Coventry Road, Southam, CV47 1QB

https://www.facebook.com/groups/1443589069276910

-

Spiritual Rainbow Church

Services on: Sundays at 18:00

The New Plough Inn, Leicester Road, Hinckley, Leicestershire LE10 1LS

https://www.facebook.com/spiritualityloveandunderstanding

-

Stafford Spiritualist Church (SNU)

Services on: Sundays at 18:30

The Barbanell Centre, 64B Co-operative Street, Stafford ST16 3DA

https://www.facebook.com/staffordspiritualistchurch.co.uk

-

Stourbridge Spiritualist Church (SNU)

Services on: Mondays at 14:30; Sunday at 18:30

49 Union Street, Stourbridge, West Midlands, DY8 1PJ

https://www.facebook.com/stourbridgespiritualistchurch

https://www.stourbridgespiritualistchurch.com

-

Sutton Coldfield Spiritualist Church (SNU)

Services on: Mondays at 13:30; Sundays at 18:30

Kenelm Road, off Manor Hill, Sutton Coldfield B73 6HD

https://www.facebook.com/Spiritualist-Church-Sutton-Coldfield-926521874064468

Tamworth National Spiritualist Church (SNU)

Services on: Wednesdays at 19:30; Sundays at 18:30

18 Marmion Street, Tamworth, Staffordshire B79 7JG

https://www.facebook.com/TamworthSNUChurch

Telford 1st Spiritualist Church (Stirchley Village Spiritualists Church) (SNU)

Services on: Saturdays at 18:30; Sundays at 18:30

St James Hall, Farm Lane, Stirchley Village, Telford, Shropshire TF3 1DY

https://www.facebook.com/TelfordFirstSNUStirchley

-

The Butterfly Fellowship

Services on: 4th Wednesday of a month at 19:30

Stourton Village Hall, Bridgnorth Rd, Stourton, Stourbridge DY7 6RT

https://www.facebook.com/butterflyfellowship

https://www.butterfly2012.com

-

The House of the Good Shepherd Christian Spiritualist Church

Services on: Sundays at 18:30

Holly Bush Walk, Hinton, Hereford HR2 6AF

https://www.facebook.com/The-House-Of-The-Good-Shepherd-Christian-Spiritualist-Church-Hereford-1311193792260218

-

Ward End Christian Spiritualist Church

Services on: Tuesdays at 14:00; Fridays at 19:30; Sundays at 18:30

Wallbank Road, Ward End, Birmingham B8 2EX

https://www.facebook.com/Wardendcsc

-

Wellington Spiritualist Church (SNU)

Services on: Sundays at 18:30

Regent St, Wellington, Telford TF1 1PQ

https://www.facebook.com/Wellington-spiritualist-Church-2021-102480818600197

-

Whomerley Spiritual Centre

Services on: 1st Saturday of a month at 19:30; alternate Sundays at 18:30

Gladstone Court Spring Drive, Stevenage, Hertfordshire SG2 8AY

https://www.facebook.com/pages/Whomerly%20Spiritualist%20Church/17759
1222357037

-

Wolverhampton Spiritualist Church (SNU)

Services on: Mondays at 13:30 and 19:30; Sunday at 18:30

67 Waterloo Road, Wolverhampton WV1 4QU

https://www.facebook.com/spiritiualistWolverhampton

http://www.wolverhamptonspiritualistchurch.org.uk

A selection of 6
Beautiful Spiritualist Prayers and Readings
On A6 Postcards

Available on Etsy:
https://www.etsy.com/uk/shop/SpiritualistGifts

Yorkshire

Ackworth Spiritual Church

Services on: Sundays at 18:30

The Parish Council Community Centre, Bell Lane, Ackworth, Pontefract WF7 7JH

https://www.facebook.com/groups/243230289111557

-

Attercliffe Spiritualist Church (SNU)

Services on: Wednesdays at 19:30; Sundays at 18:30

Bold Street, Sheffield, Attercliffe S9 2LR

https://www.facebook.com/attercliffespiritualist.church

-

Barnsley National Spiritualist Church (SNU)

Services on: Sundays at 18:15

Pitt Street West, Barnsley S701BB

https://www.facebook.com/SNUBarnsley

-

Bentley Spiritualist Centre (SNU)

Services on: Thursdays at 19:00; Sundays at 18:30

154 Askern Road, Bentley DN5 0EP

https://www.facebook.com/bentleyspiritualistchurch/

Bridlington Angel Of Light Christian Spiritualists (GW)

Services on: Thursdays at 19:00

32A South Back Lane, Bridlington YO16 4EX

https://www.facebook.com/groups/225758874256772

-

Brierley Spiritualist Church (SNU)

Services on: Sundays at 18:00

Church Street, Brierley, Barnsley, South Yorkshire S72 9HT

https://www.facebook.com/BrierleySpiritualistChurch

-

Brighouse Spiritualist Church (SNU)

Services on: Wednesdays at 19:00; Sundays at 18:30

Martin Street, Brighouse , Yorksire

https://www.facebook.com/groups/1673819356237879

-

Castleford Spiritualist Church (SNU)

Services on: Sundays at 18:30

117 Lower Oxford Street, Castleford WF10 4AQ

https://www.facebook.com/Castleford-Spiritualist-Church-140396229319778

College Road National Spiritualist Church (SNU)

Services on: Wednesdays at 19:00

College Road, Doncaster DN1 3JH

https://www.facebook.com/College-Road-National-Spiritualist-Church-Doncaster-DN1-3JH-648584501920820/

-

Doncaster Catherine Street Spiritualist Church (SNU)

Services on: Mondays at 19:00; Sundays at 18:30

Catherine Street, Doncaster, South Yorkshire DN1 3PS

https://www.facebook.com/groups/265209447620240

-

Earby and District Spiritual Group

Services on: Wednesdays at 19:30

Pensioners Centre, Linden Road, Earby, Barnoldswick BB18 6XR

https://www.facebook.com/groups/106634379418501

-

Fir Trees Spiritual Centre

Services on: Saturdays at 19:00

Fir Tree House, Spaldington, East Yorkshire DN14 7ND

https://www.facebook.com/Fir-Trees-Spiritual-Center-355591005202584

Harmony Church (International Church of St Paul)

Services on: 1st and 3rd Sundays of a month at 16:00

Harmony Country Lodge, Limestone Road, Burniston, Scarborough YO13 0DG

https://www.facebook.com/internationalchurchofstpaul

https://www.harmonychurch.co.uk

-

Harrogate Spiritualist Church

Services on: Sundays at 18:30

14 Princes Square, Harrogate HG1 1LL

https://www.facebook.com/Harrogate-Spiritual-Healing-Church-127057174092175

http://harrogatespiritualhealingchurch.co.uk

-

Hebden Bridge Spiritualist Church (SNU)

Services on: Sundays at 18:30

14 New Road, Hebden Bridge HX7 8AD

https://www.facebook.com/HebdenBridgeSpiritualistChurch

-

Hemsworth Spiritualist Church (SNU)

Services on: Mondays at 19:00

7 Grove Lane, Hemsworth, Pontefract WF9 4BB

https://www.facebook.com/groups/146678805967312

Hereafter Pioneer Spiritual Centre

Services on: Thursdays at 18:30

The Old School, Vicars Terrace, Allerton Bywater WF10 2DJ

https://www.facebook.com/groups/1003755559652004

-

Huddersfield Spiritualist Church (SNU)

Services on: Thursdays at 19:00; Sundays at 18:30

Old Leeds Road, Huddersfield, West Yorkshire HD1 1SG

https://www.facebook.com/groups/1478091905923248

-

Hull Spiritualist Church (SNU)

Services on: Sundays at 19:00

83 Folkestone Street, Hull, East Yorkshire HU5 1BJ

https://www.facebook.com/Hull-SNU-Spiritualist-Centre-1176552385838144

-

Idle Spiritualist Church (SNU)

Services on: Wednesdays at 19:00; Sundays 18:30

409 Highfield Road, Idle, Bradford BD10 8RS

https://www.facebook.com/groups/1732813850333469

-

ISA Rainbow Group

Services on: Wednesdays at 18:00

Marsh Lane Communal Hall, Arksey, Doncaster DN5 0SH

https://www.facebook.com/groups/692570991887647

Keighley Spiritualist Church (SNU)

Services on: Saturdays at 19:00

Heber Street, Keighley, West Yorkshire BD21 5JU

https://www.facebook.com/keighleyspiritualist.church

-

Knaresborough Spiritualist Society

Services on: Tuesdays at 19:15

Knaresborough House, High Street, Knaresborough HG5 0HW

https://www.facebook.com/Knaresborough-Spiritualist-Society-1582301252012462

-

Leeds Greater World Sanctuary

Services on: Sundays at 15:00

14 Clarendon Road, Leeds, West Yorkshire LS2 9NN

https://www.facebook.com/Leeds-greater-world-sanctuary-466051883575429

-

Mexborough Spiritualist Church (SNU)

Services on: Sundays at 18:30

Bank Street, Mexborough, South Yorkshire S64 9LL

https://www.facebook.com/MexboroughSpiritualistChurch

http://mexboroughspiritualist.church

-

Middlesborough Spiritualist Church (SNU)

Services on: Thursdays at 19:00; Sundays at 18:30

115 Borough Road, Middlesborough, North Yorkshire TS1 3AN

https://www.facebook.com/groups/1747224162160699

-

Moorends Spiritualist Church (SNU)

Services on: Thursdays at 19:00; Sundays at 18:00

Newholme Drive, Moorends, Doncaster, South Yorkshire DN8 4TB

https://www.facebook.com/moorendsspiritualistchurch

-

Morley Spiritualist Church (SNU)

Services on: Tuesdays at 15:00 and 19:00; Sundays at 18:30

Zoar Street, Morley, Leeds, West Yorkshire LS27 8JB

https://www.facebook.com/groups/1228382650556047

-

Normanton Spiritualist Centre (SNU)

Services on: Sundays at 18:30

Normanton Spiritualist Centre, Back Oxford Street, Normanton WF6 1QE

https://www.facebook.com/groups/560777420620555

-

Ossett Spiritualist Church (SNU)

Services on: Wednesdays at 19:00; Sundays at 18:30

Broadheads Yard, Ventnor Way, Ossett, Yorkshire WF5 8PA

https://www.facebook.com/groups/628705287202265

Otley Spiritualist Church (SNU)

Services on: Saturdays at 19:00; Sundays at 18:30

36 New Market, Otley, Leeds LS21 3AE

https://www.facebook.com/OtleySNUChurch

-

Parkgate Spiritualist Church (SNU)

Services on: Sundays at 19:00

2 Ashwood Road, Parkgate, Rotherham S62 6HT

https://www.facebook.com/Parkgate-Spiritualist-Church-SNU-414609525297406

-

Quarmby Spiritualist Church (SNU)

Services on: Sundays at 18:15

Harp Road, Quarmby, Huddersfield HD3 4HH

https://www.facebook.com/quarmbysnu

http://quarmbyspiritualistchurch.co.uk

-

Rotherham Spiritualist Church – Percy Street (SNU)

Services on: Sundays at 18:30

Percy Street, Rotherham S65 1ED

https://www.facebook.com/groups/121254897987811

-

Scarborough National Spiritualist Church (SNU)

Services on: Tuesdays at 14:15

Small Meeting Room, The Library, Vernon Road, Scarborough, North Yorkshire YO11 2NN

https://www.facebook.com/groups/194259415193222

-

Sheffield Darnell Spiritualist Church (SNU)

Services on: Sundays at 18:30

315 Shirland Lane, Sheffield S9 3FN

https://www.facebook.com/Spiritualist-church-Darnall-960675150686802

-

Sheffield South Road Spiritualist Church (SNU)

Services on: Mondays at 19:00

South Road – Corner of Fir Street, Sheffield, South Yorkshire S6 3TA

https://www.facebook.com/sheffieldsouthroad

-

Sheffield Whitham Road Spiritualist Church (SNU)

Services on: Sundays at 15:00

109 Whitham Road Sheffield S10 2SL

https://www.facebook.com/groups/174768449232308

-

South Elmsall Spiritualist Church (SNU)

Services on: Saturdays at 18:30

29 Church St, South Elmsall, Pontefract WF9 2JE

https://www.facebook.com/groups/1099172453473371

Sowerby Bridge Spiritualist Church (SNU)

Services on: Sundays at 18:00

Hollins Lane, Sowerby Bridge, West Yorkshire HX6 2RX

https://www.facebook.com/sowerbybridgespiritualistchurch

-

Spiritual Journey's

Services on: Sundays at 18:30

Colton Institute, Meynell Road, Leeds LS15 9AQ

https://www.facebook.com/spirtualifejourneys

-

Stainforth Spiritualist Church (SNU)

Services on: Sundays at 18:30

Station Road, Stainforth, Doncaster DN7 5QB

https://www.facebook.com/profile.php?id=100069361800692

Victoria Road Independent Spiritualist Church

Services on: aiming to re-open after Easter

5 Victoria Road, Bridlington YO15 2BW

https://www.facebook.com/BridlingtonIndependentSpiritualistChurch

---

Wakefield Spiritualist Church (SNU)

Services on: Mondays at 19:00

18 Peterson Road, Wakefield, West Yorkshire WF1 4EB

https://www.facebook.com/groups/211704776801594/

Warmsworth & Edlington Spiritualist Church (SNU)

Services on: Thursdays at 19:00; Sundays at 18:00

Edlington Lane, Warmsworth DN4 9LT

https://www.facebook.com/Warmsworth-Edlington-Spiritualist-Church-1916088522012846

‗

Wath & West Melton Spiritualist Church (SNU)

Services on: Sundays at 18:45

6 Barnsley Road, Wath on Dearne, Rotherham, South Yorkshire S63 6PY

https://www.facebook.com/WandWMSC

-

Wombwell Spiritualist Church (SNU)

Services on: Sundays at 18:30

Kelvin Grove, Wombwell, Barnsley, South Yorkshire S73 0DL

https://www.facebook.com/Wombwell-spiritualist-church-117192496331179

-

York Group of Spiritualists

Services on: Sundays at 19:00

The Old School, Mill Lane, Wigginton, York YO32 2PU

https://www.facebook.com/groups/1644809905756361

-

York Spiritualist Centre (SNU)

Services on: Sundays at 11:00

7-9 Wilton Rise, Holgate, York YO24 4BT

https://www.facebook.com/groups/270018781481639/

Yorkshire Spiritualist Association

Services on: Sundays at 18:00

Quaker Meeting House, 188 Woodhouse Lane, Leeds LS2 9DX

https://www.facebook.com/Yorkshire-Spiritualist-Association-1927990364137477

Love Light Grows

On stony paths,
On seas of green,
Love light grows.
On mountains high,
On rivers deep,
Love light grows.
On hearts of stone,
And souls of greed,
Love light grows.
On bodies of pain,
On hearts of grief,
Love light enfolds.
On minds of light,
On souls of peace,
Love light blossoms.
Through the phases of life,
Through the evolution of self,
Love light grows.

By Veronica Jenkins

Further links

Spiritualist National Union
https://www.facebook.com/thespiritualistsnationalunion
https://www.snu.org.uk/

The Greater World
https://www.greaterworld.net/

Advertising Page for Spiritualist Venues to post their events
https://www.facebook.com/groups/spiritualistchurchservices

List of what Spiritualist events on each day
https://www.facebook.com/groups/onlinespiritualchurchservices
If you would like this list sent to you each day on messenger, WhatsApp or by email Subscription is £5 per month from
https://findmeamedium.com/membership-join/

Spiritualist Gifts (Postcards with Inspired Poetry, readings and prayers)
https://www.etsy.com/uk/shop/SpiritualistGifts

NFTs – ownership gives access to subscription areas of
https://findmeamedium.com/

https://opensea.io/collection/spiritualistmedium-collection

If you are a platform medium wanting to be added to a list available to Churches and centres please complete the online form

https://findmeamedium.com/gdpr/

If you know of any other Spiritualist venues that are open please email me on findmeamedium@gmail.com or

find me on FB https://www.facebook.com/findmeamedium1/

Prayer of Closing

Thank you Great and Holy Spirit for the love that has been shared this day.

May we take that love into our lives so we can share it with others through healing.

May the blessings Angels have shared with us, surround us and keep us safe.

Safe in the knowledge of eternal life,

The understanding of spiritual progress through our actions for others

And our shared responsibility in the protection and support of those that need it.

May that love protect us from the evils within us and outside of us until we can meet again.

Blessings Be.

By Veronica Jenkins 2021

To have your organisation advertised in the next edition of this book please contact findmeamedium@gmail.com

Completed with moral support of my wonderful husband Paul

Printed in Great Britain
by Amazon